Music Monographs in Series

A Bibliography of Numbered Monograph
Series in the Field of Music Current Since 1945

by

Fred Blum

The Scarecrow Press, Inc.
New York & London   1964

Copyright 1964 by

Fred Blum

L. C. Catalog Card No. 64-11794

To Rita and Arthur Benton

Preface

The purpose of this bibliography is to assist music librarians in controlling and expanding their holdings of numbered monograph series in the field of music; to make it easier for acquisitions librarians to order, catalogers to catalog, and readers to utilize the growing literature available in this format; to suggest that time and money might be saved by placing such material on continuation order; to encourage the filing of series entries in public catalogs; to suggest the possibility of shelving at least some series as units; and to call attention to the need for similar bibliographies in other subject areas.

Over 250 series in which at least one volume has appeared since 1945 are included here. They come from about thirty countries and are written in a score of languages, German (about 35 per cent), English (about 18 per cent), Italian, French, Czech and Slovak, Polish, Flemish and Dutch, a bi- and multi-lingual group, Spanish, Hungarian, Swedish, Bulgarian, Danish, Finnish, Latin, Norwegian, Portuguese, and Yugoslav.

The series fall more-or-less entirely within the Library of Congress' (hereafter "LC") Music Literature (ML) and/or Music Theory (MT) classifications. Over one-third of them may best be described as broadly musicological in content, many issued under the auspices of universities or scholarly soceietes; others, ranging in tone from the academic to the popular, cover the gamut of musical subject matter in the specific areas of biography, music theory, music education, bibliography, contemporary music, jazz and popular music, sacred music, instruments, studies concerning a specific composer, ethnomusicology, opera, and phonorecords (in order of frequency).

Series entries include: (1) title, (2) editor or issuing organization (if not implicit in the title), (3) place of publication, (4) publisher, and (5) supplementary notes (optional).

Series have been entered alphabetically by title. In a few cases, where the title does not suffice to distinguish a series, the entry is under the name of the issuing organization. If the LC entry differs from ours, the "Index to Series and Issuing Organizations" includes appropriate cross-references and also, after our own entry, the full LC form, introduced by an asterisk (e.g., Neue Studien zur Musikwissenschaft. *Akademie der Wissenschaften und der Literatur, Mainz. Kommission für Musikwissenschaft. Neue Studien zur Musikwissenschaft.). Unless the LC entry is under the geographical location, however, it has not been deemed necessary to include cross-references to cities, states, or countries.

If the name of an issuing institution appears on the title-page, it is included in the "Index to Series and Issuing Organizations," but if an individual is named as editor, he is cited in the "Index of Names." Place of publication (city) is given in the language of the source; for English usage, consult the list of "Publishers and Their Agents." Such notes as "partly numbered" (if not all of the volumes in a series are numbered), "partly music" (if scores, as well as monographs, are included), "mostly transl." ("mostly translations"), and "ceased pub." ("ceased publication") may be added to the series entry as appropriate. Since series have a way of lying dormant for a long time, only to revive again after being given up for dead, "ceased pub." is used sparingly.

The entries for the individual volumes include (1) author, editor, or other main entry, (2) title and subtitle, (3) important descriptive information (optional), (4) edition(s) and date(s) of publication, and (5) supplementary notes (optional).

Names of authors are given in inverted form, with

initials only. Fuller names of authors, editors, translators, and other contributors, together with personal names appearing in the titles, may be found in the "Index of Names," which also provides important variant spellings and cross-references. To the best of our knowledge, except for some standardization of punctuation and other minor discrepancies that could not be avoided in a study which relies so heavily on secondary sources (national bibliographies, library catalogs, correspondence with publishers), titles are rendered as they appear on the title-page. Publication dates, whatever their source, are entered without brackets. If we have reason to be uncertain about a date, a question mark is added. If the appearance of a title has not been confirmed, no date is given. The term "in prep." ("in preparation") has been used to cover everything from "in prep. as of 19--" to "in prep. for 1966."

Capitalization follows the normal usage for each of the various languages. For the sake of visual clarity in the series headings only, however, in the Romance, Slavic, and Finno-Ugrian languages capitals are used for all important words in the names of societies and publishing firms, and for the first important word after initial articles and the terms "Collection" and "Colección." For typographical reasons, Polish hooks have been replaced by cedillas and klickas by breves; otherwise, accents follow the normal usage in the respective languages.

In the present edition, it has been necessary to exclude unnumbered series, non-monographic material (periodicals, congress reports, miscellanea musicologica), musical scores and facsimiles of scores, series containing phonorecords, self-terminating series, general cultural and interdisciplinary publications, and works primarily devoted to such related fields as liturgy, folklore, theater, and the dance. Only a sampling of opera librettos could be included.

The following list of unnumbered series current in Paris alone since 1945 suggests the quantity of publication in just one of these formats (series marked with an asterisk are among the most important French contributions to musicological research): Amour de la musique (Éd. Le Bon Plaisir): *Bibliothèque internationale de musicologie (Presses Universitaires de France); Bibliothèque musicale (Richard-Masse); Les Cahiers de la musique française (Didier); *Le Choeur des muses (Centre National de la Recherche Scientifique); Coll. l'Enfant musicien (Expansion Musicale); Coll. Enseignement musical (Lemoine); Enseignement rationnel de la musique (Expansion Musicale); La Flûte de Pan (J.-B. Janin); Formes, écoles et oeuvres musicales (Larousse); Coll. les Grands musiciens (Horay); Grands musiciens racontés aux enfants (Nathan); Coll. des Guides musicaux (Les Belles-Lettres); Coll. Harmoniques (Éd. France-Empire); Histoire de la musique (A. Colin); Jeunesse de la musique (Amiot-Dumont); Coll. les Maîtres de la musique (Le Bon Plaisir); Coll. Musicale (Laffont); Coll. les Musiciens célèbres (Laurens); Coll. Musiciens d'aujourd'hui (Ventadour); Coll. Musiciens d'hier et d'aujourd'hui (L'Inter); Coll. Musique (Corrêa); La Musique dans la civilisation (Aubier); Musique et musiciens (Soc. d'Ed. Françaises et Internationales); Coll. Musique sacrée (Le Roux); Coll. Nos amis les musiciens (E.I.S.E.); Coll. Paroles sans musique (Ventadour); Coll. Plaisir de connaître (Expansion Musicale); Coll. Pour la musique (Gallimard); *Publications de l'Institut de Musicologie de l'Université de Paris; Le Revue musicale: les carnets critiques (Richard-Masse); Coll. Rythmes (La Revue Moderne); Coll. la Vie des grands musiciens (G.-T. Rageot); and *Coll. la Vie musicale en France sous les rois bourbons (Picard). Of course, the French have no monopoly on this format, as the significant series now in progress under the joint auspices of the American Musicological Society and the Music Library Association attests.

For information about periodicals one can turn to such specialized works as Eckart Rohlfs's Die deutschsprachigen

Musikperiodica 1945-1957 (Regensburg: Bosse, 1961) and
James B. Coover's "A Bibliography of East European Music
Periodicals" (in Fontes Artis Musicae, beginning with
1956/2), as well as the Union List of Serials (3rd ed. in
progress) and New Serial Titles (especially the Classed Subject Arrangement). Since 1949, The Music Index (Detroit:
Information Service, Inc.) has provided an index to an ever-
increasing number of music journals.

Marie Briquet indexes international congress reports of
an earlier period in La musique dans les congrès internationaux (1835-1939) (Paris: Société Française de Musicologie,
1961). Especially worthy of note in this category are the
reports of the International Musicological Society and the
International Association of Music Libraries:

Internationale Gesellschaft für Musikwissenschaft;
Société internationale de musicologie; International
Musicological Society. Kongressbericht; Compte rendu;
Report.
Briquet Nos. 78-81 indexes Nos. 1-4; there fol-
low 5th, Utrecht, 1952 (published 1953); 6th, Oxford, 1955 (unpub.); 7th, Köln, 1958 (1959); 8th,
N.Y., 1961 (Papers, 1961; Reports, 1962); 9th,
Salzburg, 1964 (in prep.).
Association internationale des bibliothèques musicales;
Internationale Vereinigung der Musikbibliotheken; International Association of Music Libraries. Congrès
international des bibliothèques musicales. Actes.
1st, Firenze, 1949 (unpub.); 2nd, Lüneburg, 1950
(1951); 3rd, Paris, 1951 (1953); 4th, Bruxelles,
1955 (=Fontes Artis Musicae, 1956/1); 5th, Cam-
bridge, 1959 (=Hinrichsen's Eleventh Music Book,
1961); 6th, Stockholm, 1962 (in Fontes Artis
Musicae, 1964/1); 7th, Aarhus, 1964.

The reports of the Congrès international de musique sacrêe,
Congresso internazionale di musica, Internationaler Kon-

gress für katholische Kirchenmusik, and the Internationaler
Kongress für die Berufliche Ausbildung der Musiker might
also be mentioned, along with such national reports as the
Berichte of the Gesellschaft für Musikforschung (Germany)
and the Crónica of the Congreso nacional de música sagrada
(Spain).

Even the briefest select list of miscellanea musicologica
would have to include the Darmstädter Beiträge zur Neuen
Musik (Schott); Hinrichsen's Music Books (Hinrichsen);
Hudobnovedné Štúdie (Slovenská Akadémia Vied); Miscellanea
musicologica (Prague, Katedra dějin hudby na fil.-hist.
fakulté Karlovy university); Musik des Ostens: Sammelbände
für historische und vergleichende Forschung (Bärenreiter);
Musikologie: sborník pro hudební vědu a kritiku (SNKLHU);
Prace Naukowe Instytutu Muzykologii (Universytet Warszawski); Studia Muzykologiczne (PWM); and Studien zur Musikwissenschaft: Beihefte der Denkmäler der Tonkunst in
Österreich (Böhlau et al). Recent Soviet contributions in this
format include Muzykal'noe nasledstvo; sborniki po istorii
muzykal'noĭ kul'tury SSSR (Moscow, 1962-), Voprosy
muzykoznaniia (Moscow, 1953/54-), and the following publications of the music conservatories:

Leningrad. Gos. Konservatoriia. Kafedra teorii muzyki.
Ocherki po teoreticheskomu muzykoznaniiu. 1959- .
L'vov. Gos. Konservatoriia imeni Lysenko. Nauchno
zapiski. 1957- .
Minsk. Belorusskaia gos. Konservatoriia. Nauchno-
metodicheskie zapiski. 1958- .
Novosibirsk. Gos. Konservatoriia. Nauchno-metodiches-
kie zapiski. 1958- .
Saratov. Gos. Konservatoriia. Nauchno-metodicheskie
zapiski. 1959- .
Sverdlovsk. Ural'skaia gos. Konservatoriia imeni M. P.
Musorgskogo. Nauchno-metodicheskie zapiski. 1957- .
Anna H. Heyer's Historical Sets, Collected Editions,
and Monuments of Music; A Guide to Their Contents

(Chicago: American Library Association, 1957; 2nd edition
in progress) and the articles by Wolfgang Schmieder on
"Denkmäler der Tonkunst" and "Gesamtausgaben" in Die
Musik in Geschichte und Gegenwart may be consulted for
information about scores in series. E. A. Baer's Titles in
Series; A Handbook for Librarians and Students
(The Scarecrow Press, 1953 and supplements) lists a number of general cultural and academic series that include,
among other things, occasional volumes about music.

Acknowledgments

It has been my good fortune to have the assistance of
a large number of publishers, librarians, and other friends
and colleagues in the preparation of this bibliography. Since
the list of publishers has grown so long, I must content my-
self with observing that many of the firms and societies
listed under the heading of "Publishers and Their Agents" con-
tributed far more in the way of typewritten and printed
material than their commercial interests alone would have
required.

Among the librarians, I am especially indebted to M.
François Lesure (Bibliothèque Nationale, Paris), Dr. Cari
Johansson (Kungl. Musikaliska Akademiens Bibliotek, Stock-
holm), Herr H.-M. Plesske (Deutsche Bücherei, Leipzig),
Señor Don Justo García Morales (Servicio de Informacíon
Documental y Bibliográfica, Biblioteca Nacional, Madrid),
and the Director of the Centro Nazionale di Informazioni
Bibliografiche (Biblioteca Nazionale Centrale Vittorio
Emanuele II, Rome) for graciously supplying information
based on their own collections. Dr. Harold E. Samuel of
Cornell University generously supplied a copy of a mimeo-
graphed list of monograph series that he had prepared for
one of his courses, and Dr. Otto E. Albrecht of the University of Pennsylvania made his card file of similar information available to me.

For kindly proofreading the entries in their special

languages, the author is indebted to the following scholars at the Library of Congress: Dr. Barbara Krader (now at Syracuse University) and Dr. Zorka Černá (Czech and Slovak), Dr. Janina W. Hoskins (Polish), and Dr. Elemer Bako (Finno-Ugrian).

For access to their magnificant catalogs, and for useful suggestions, the author would like to thank Mrs. Virginia Cunningham (Head of the Descriptive Cataloging Division's Music Cataloging Section) and the staffs of the Card Division and Serial Record Division.

Last, but definitely not least, by his advice and encouragement, especially during the formative stages of this project, Mr. Edward N. Waters (Assistant Chief, Music Division, Library of Congress) made a major contribution, for which the author is deeply grateful.

Table of Contents

Publishers and Their Agents

AMP. See Associated Music Publishers.

Accademia Musicale Chigiana, via di Città 89, Siena, Italy.
Agent: Ticci.

Akadémiai Kiadó, Alkotmány utca 21, Budapest 5, Hungary.
Agent: Kultura.

Akademische Druck- und Verlagsanstalt, Auersperggasse
12, Graz, Austria.

Walter C. Allen, P. O. Box 501, Stanhope, New Jersey.

Allgemeiner Cäcilien-Verband, Burgmauer 1, Köln, Germany.

Almqvist & Wiksells Boktryckeri, Box 96, 26 Gamla
Brogatan, Stockholm C, Sweden.

Amalthea-Verlag, Schwarzenbergplatz 10, Vienna 4, Austria.

Amerbach-Verlag, Basel, Switzerland. Amerbach-Musikbibliothek not available.

American Institute of Musicology (Rome), P. O. Box 30665,
Dallas 25, Texas.

American Musicological Society. Dr. Otto E. Albrecht,
Business Manager, 204 Hare Building, University of
Pennsylvania, Philadelphia 4, Pennsylvania.
Agent: Galaxy. Continental agent: Bärenreiter.

Arcadia-Verlag, Heimhuder Str. 36, 2000 Hamburg 13,
Germany.

Ars Polona, Krakowskie Przedmieście 7, Warsaw, Poland.

Artia, P. O. Box 790, Ve Smečkách 30, Prague, Czechoslovakia.

Associated Music Publishers, Inc. , 1 West 47th Street,
New York 36, N. Y.

Associazione Italiana Santa Cecilia per la Musica Sacra,
via della Scrofa 70, Rome, Italy.

Editrice Athena, Milan, Italy.

Baerenreiter Music Publishers, Inc., P.O. Box 115, Inwood Station, New York, N.Y. 10034.

Bärenreiter-Verlag, Heinrich-Schütz-Allee 29-37, 3500 Kassel-Wilhelmshöhe, Germany.

Casa Editrice Il Balcone, via Sandri 2, Milan, Italy.

Beethovenhaus, Bonngasse 18, Bonn, Germany.

Société d'Éditions Les Belles Lettres, 95, boulevard Raspail, Paris 6, France.

Éditions du Belvédère, Paris, France.

Bibliotheca, Budapest. Agent: Kultura.

Bielefelder Verlagsanstalt, Postfach 1140, Schillerplatz 20, 4800 Bielefeld, Germany.

A. & C. Black Ltd., 4-6 Soho Square, London W.1, England.

Casa Editrice Fratelli Bocca, via Monte del Gallo 86, Milan, Italy. Agent: Feltrinelli.

Verlag Hermann Böhlaus Nachfolger, Frankgasse 4, Vienna 9, Austria.

Boosey & Hawkes, Kronprinzenstr. 26, 5300 Bonn, Germany. U.S.: Boosey, N.Y.

Boosey & Hawkes, Inc., 30 West 57th Street, New York 19, N.Y.

Gustav Bosse Verlag, Landshuter Str. 14B, 8400 Regensburg, Germany.

H. Bouvier und Co. Verlag, Postfach 346, Am Hof 32, 5300 Bonn, Germany.

Breitkopf und Härtel, Karlstr. 10, Leipzig C 1, GDR. U.S. : AMP.

Breitkopf und Härtel, Postfach 74, Burgstr. 6, 6200 Wiesbaden 1, Germany. U.S.: AMP.

E.J. Brill, Oude Rijn 33a, Leiden, Holland.

Bŭlgarska Akademiia na Naukite, Instituta za Muzika, Sofia, Bulgaria.

Georg D.W. Callwey Verlag, Finkenstr. 2, 8000 Munich, Germany.

Cassell & Company Ltd., 35 Red Lion Square, London W.C.

1, England.

Catholic University of America Press, 620 Michigan Ave., N. E., Washington 17, D. C.

Centre Belge de Documentation Musicale (CEBEDEM), 3, rue du Commerce, Brussels, Belgium. U. S. : Elkan.

Centro de Estudios Folclóricos y Musicales, Universidad Nacional de Colombia, Bogotá, Colombia.

Centro di Studi Palestriniani, Rome, Italy.

Éditions du Cervin, Ch. Métairie 19, Pully, Lausanne 19, Switzerland.

Chanticleer Company, Inc., 424 Madison Ave., New York 17, N. Y.

Church Music Society. Agent: Oxford. U. S. : Oxford, N. Y.

Colloques de Wégimont, Cercle International d'Études Ethno-Musicologiques, 77, rue des Trois Tilleuls, Brussels 17, Belgium.

La Colombe, Éditions du Vieux Colombier, 5, rue Rousse-let, Paris 7, France.

Columbia University Press, 2960 Broadway, New York 27, N. Y.

Composers' Guild of Great Britain, 5 Egmont House, 116 Shaftesbury Avenue, London W. 1., England.

Consejo Superior de Investigaciones Científicas, Vitrubio 16, Madrid, Spain. See also: Instituto Español de Musicología.

Éditions du Coudrier, 20, rue Delambre, Paris 14, France.

A. B. Creyghton, 45 Lassuslaan, Bilthoven, Holland.

W. Crüwell Verlagsbuchhandlung, Postfach 207, Olpe 29, 4600 Dortmund 1, Germany.

Dabo-Peranić Éditeur, 30 rue Jacob, Paris, France. No pub. avail.

Daisan Shobô, 6, Sarugaku-cho 2-chome, Kanda, Chiyoda-ku, Tokyo, Japan.

Deutsche Verlag für Musik, Karlstr. 10, Leipzig C 1, GDR. Agent: Schott. U. S. : AMP.

Dirección General de Relaciones Culturales, Plaza de la Provincia 1, Madrid, Spain.

3

A. Drago, via Roma 58, Magenta (Milano), Italy.

Ferd. Dümmlers Verlag, Postfach 297, Kaiserstr. 31-37, 5300 Bonn, Germany.

E. M. I. Electronics Ltd., Sales and Service, Blyth Road, Hayes, Middlesex, England.

Henri Elkan, 1316 Walnut St., Philadelphia 7, Pennsylvania.

Elsevier, Mercelisstraat 74, Brussels, Belgium.

Essential Books, Inc., Fair Lawn, New Jersey. Agent: Oxford. U. S.: Oxford, N. Y.

Éditions Européa, 21, rue des Champs, Strasbourg-Wendenheim (Bas-Rhin), France.

Editrice Faro, via Po 21a, Rome, Italy.

Editore Feltrinelli, via Andegari 6, Milan, Italy.

Fischbacher, 33, rue de Seine, Paris 6, France.

Éditions Fleurus, 31-33, rue de Fleurus, Paris 6, France.

Fortress Press, 2900 Queen Lane, Philadelphia, Pennsylvania.

Fountain Press Ltd., 46-47 Chancery Lane, London W. C. 2, England.

Franco Colombo, Inc., 16 West 61st St., New York 23, N. Y.

Casa Editrice Federico Fussi, via G. Pascoli 9, Florence, Italy.

W. Gaade, Grote Marktstraat 39, The Hague, Holland.

Galaxy Music Corporation, 2121 Broadway, New York 23, N. Y.

Librairie Gallimard, 5, rue Sébastien-Bottin, Paris 7, France.

Friedrich Gennrich, Südliche Ringstr. 256, Langen bei Frankfurt, Germany.

Verlag der Gesellschaft zur Förderung der systematischen Musikwissenschaft e. V., Feldstr. 22, Düsseldorf, Germany.

Hans Geyer, Münzwardeingasse 6, Vienna 2, Austria.

Gondolat Kiadó, Bródy Sándor utca 16, Budapest 8, Hungary. Agent: Kultura.

J. H. Gottmer, Postbus 555, Haarlem, Holland.

The H. W. Gray Company, 159 East 48th St., New York 17, N. Y.

Gregorian Institute of America, 2132 Jefferson Avenue, Toledo 2, Ohio.

Ugo Guanda, via Cantelli 13, Parma, Italy.

Wilhelm Hansen, Gothersgade 9/11, Copenhagen, Denmark. U. S.: G. Schirmer.

Verlag Der Harmonikalehrer, Trossingen/Württemburg, Germany.

Paul Haupt, Falkenplatz 11 & 14, Bern, Switzerland.

Rudolf Haupt, Hillerse 70 über Northeim Hannover, Germany.

P. H. Heitz, 16, rue du Maréchal-Joffre, Strasbourg (Bas-Rhin), France.

G. Henle Verlag, Schongauer Str. 24, 8000 Munich 55, Germany. U. S.: Roundelay.

Herder & Co., Wollzeile 33, Vienna 1, Austria.

Max Hesses Verlag, Joachim-Friedrich-Str. 38, 1000 Berlin-Halensee 31; also Maximilianstr. 9, 8592 Wunsiedel, Germany.

Heugel et Cie, 2 bis, rue Vivienne, Paris 2, France. U. S.: Presser.

Éditions de l'Heure, Monté-Carlo, Monaco.

A. J. Heuwekemeyer, Bredeweg 21, Amsterdam, Holland.

Johann Philipp Hinnenthal-Verlag, Heinrich-Schutz-Allee 35, 3500 Kassel-Wilhelmshöhe, Germany. Agent: Bärenreiter.

Hinrichsen Edition Ltd., Bach House, 10-12 Baches St., London N. 1, England. U. S.: Peters.

Hörsta Förlag AB., Värtavägen 55, Stockholm, Sweden.

Friedrich Hofmeister Musikverlag, Karlstr. 10, Leipzig C 1, GDR. Agent: Musia, Forsthausstr. 101, Frankfurt am Main, Germany.

Friedrich Hofmeister, Eppsteiner Str. 43, 6000 Frankfurt am Main 1, Germany.

Heinrich Hohler Verlag, Breslauer Str. 9, 8910 Landsberg
am Lech, Germany.

Matth. Hohner, Postfach 160, Hohnerstr., 7217 Trossingen
/Württemberg, Germany.

Brüder Hollinek, Steingasse 25, Vienna 3, Austria.

Hudebni Matice. Agent: Artia.

Hug & Co., Limmatquai 26-28, Zurich, Switzerland. U.S.:
Peters.

The Hymn Society of America, 475 Riverside Drive, New
York 27, N.Y.

Imprenta Universitaria, Estado 63, Santiago, Chile.

Information Service, Inc., 10 West Warren St., Detroit 1,
Michigan.

Institute of Mediaeval Music, 1653 West 8th St., Brooklyn,
New York 11223.

Instituto Español de Musicología, Egipciacas 15, Barcelona
1, Spain.

Institutt for Musikkvitenskap, Universitetet i Oslo, Oslo,
Norway. Agents: Universitetsforlaget; H. Lyche.

Instituut vor Muziekwetenschap der Rijksuniversiteit te
Utrecht, Rijnkade la, Utrecht, Holland.

Internationale Vereinigung der Musikbibliotheken, Sekretariat,
Ständeplatz 16, Kassel, Germany.

Istituto d'Alta Cultura, via Fatebenefratelli 5, Milan, Italy.

Istituto Editoriale Italiano, via B. Quaranta 58/21, Milan,
Italy.

Jazz Publications, Postfach 736, Basel 1, Switzerland.

Jeunesses Musicales de Belgique, 11, rue Baron Horta,
Brussels, Belgium.

Verlag Junge Musik, Schott. See Schott.

Verlag Paul Kaltschmid, Gymnasiumstr. 40, Vienna 18,
Austria.

Éditions René Kister, 33, Quai Wilson, Geneva, Switzerland.

Krajské Nakladatelství, Dimitrovova ul. 28, Ostrava,
Czechoslovakia. Agent: Artia.

Musikverlag Ludwig Krenn, Reindorfgasse 42, Vienna 15,

Austria.

J. Philip Kruseman, Nassauplein 1B, The Hague, Holland.

Kultura, Népköztársaság útja 21, Budapest 6, Hungary.

Kungl. Musikaliska. See Musikaliska.

Verlag der Kunst, Kipsdorferstr. 93, Dresden A. 21,
GDR.

Kustannustalo, Mikonkatu 11A, Helsinki, Finland.

Editorial Labor, Provenza 84-88, Barcelona, Spain.

J. B. Lippincott Company, East Washington Square, Philadelphia 5, Pennsylvania.

Éditions Lire, 59, faub. Montmélian, Chambèry, France.

H. Lyche. U. S.: Peters.

The Macmillan Company, 60 Fifth Avenue, New York 11,
N. Y.

Richard Masse, 7, place St. Sulpice, Paris 6, France.

Merlin Press, 250 West 57th Street, New York, 19, N. Y.
Agent: Baerenreiter, N. Y.

Verlag Merseburger, Postfach 25, Alemannenstr. 20,
1000 Berlin-Nikolassee 38; also Hindenburgstr. 42,
Darmstadt 16, Germany. U. S.: Peters.

Messaggerie Musicale, 2/4 galleria del Corso, Milan,
Italy.

Mitteldeutscher Verlag, Robert-Blum-Str. 37, Halle/Saale,
GDR.

Karl Heinrich Möseler Verlag, Postfach 460, Hoffman-von-
Fallersleben-Str. 8, 3340 Wolfenbüttel, Germany. U. S.:
Presto.

Mondial-Verlag Hans Gerig, Drususgasse 7/11, 5000
Cologne 1, Germany. Agent: Volk.

La Casa Editrice Monsalvato. Agent: Fussi.

The Moravian Music Foundation, Inc., 20 Cascade Ave.,
Winston-Salem, North Carolina.

Willy Müller, Süddeutscher Musikverlag, Märzgasse 5,
6900 Heidelberg, Germany.

Müller-Thiergarten-Verlag, Heidelberg, Germany.

Museo Histórico Nacional, Sección de Musicología, Montevideo, Uruguay.

Kungl. Musikaliska Akademiens Bibliotek, Postbox 16265, Stockholm 16, Sweden.

Verlag Das Musikinstrument, Klüberstr. 9, Frankfurt am Main, Germany.

J. Muusses Drukkerij, Postbus 13, Kerkstraat 20-23, Purmerend, Holland.

Verlag National-Zeitung. See Papillons-Verlag.

Naucna Kniga, Izdavacko Preduzece Nr Srbije, Knez Mihajlova 40, Belgrade, Yugoslavia.

Nederland's Boekhuis, Parkstraat 16, Tilburg, Holland.

De Nederlandsche Boekhandel, 7, Sint-Jacobsmarkt, Antwerp, Belgium.

Neuzeit Verlag, Karlstr. 124, Munich, Germany.

Arthur Niggli, Teufen/Appenzel, Switzerland. Agent : Tiranti.

Nordiska Musikförlaget, Pipersgatan 29, Stockholm K, Sweden.

Noord-Hollandsche Uitgevers Maatschappij, Postbus 103, Amsterdam, Holland.

Novello & Co. Ltd., 160 Wardour St., London W. 1, England. U. S.: Gray.

Editorial Nueva Visión, Cerrito 1371, Buenos Aires, Argentina.

The Oakwood Press, Tandridge Lane, Lingfield, Surrey England.

Oesterreichischer Bundesverlag, Schwarzenbergstr. 5, Vienna 1, Austria. U. S.: AMP.

Oliva-Verlag, Postfach 60, Kaemmererplatz 2, 2190 Cuxhaven, Germany.

Casa Editrice Leo S. Olschki, casella postale 295, via delle Caldaie 14, Florence, Italy.

Nakladatelství Orbis, Vinohrady, Stalinova tř. 46, Prague, 2, Czech. Agent: Artia.

Oxford University Press, Music Department, 44 Conduit St., London W. 1, England. U. S.: Oxford, N. Y.

Oxford University Press, Inc., 417 Fifth Ave., New York

8

16, N. Y.

PWM. See Polskie Wydawnictwo Muzyczny.

Edizione Palatine di R. Pezzani, Torino, Italy.

Division of Music and Visual Arts, Pan American Union, 17th St. between Constitution and C, Washington, D. C. Agent: Southern.

Państwowa Wyższa Szkoła Muzyczna, Katowice, Poland.

Panton, Nakladatelství Svazu Čs. Skladatelů, Malá Strana, Besední ul. 3, Prague, Czech. Agent: Artia.

Papillons-Verlag, Schanzweg 64, Basel, Switzerland.

Max Parrish & Co. Ltd., 55 Queen Anne St., London W. 1, England. U. S.: Chanticleer.

Pazdirkovo Nakl. Brno. Agent: Artia.

Verlag Adalbert Pechans Witwe, Laudongasse 10, Vienna 8, Austria.

Pegasus Verlag, Postfach 68, Krämerstr. 19, 6330 Wetzlar, Germany.

Pergamon Press Ltd., Headington Hill Hall, Oxford, England.

C. F. Peters Corporation, 373 Park Avenue South, New York 16, N. Y.

Phoenix House Ltd., 10-13 Bedford St., London W. C. 2, England.

Polskie Wydawnictwo Muzyczne, Al. Krasińskiego 11, Cracow, Poland.

Theodore Presser Company, Presser Place, Bryn Mawr, Pennsylvania.

Presto Music Service, Box 10704, Tampa, Florida.

Friedrich Pustet, Gutenbergstr. 8, 8400 Regensburg, Germany.

Quelle & Meyer, Schloss-Wolfsbrunnen-Weg 29, Postfach 1340, 6900 Heidelberg 1, Germany.

Rams Skull Press, Ferntree Gully, Australia.

Revue Disques, 59, rue La Fayette, Paris, France.

Der Rheingold-Verlag, Rheinallee 17, Mainz, Germany.

Musikantiquariat Ricke. See Verlag Walter Ricke.

Verlag Walter Ricke, Türkenstr. 15a, Munich 2, Germany.

G. Ricordi, via Berchet 2, Milan, Italy. U.S.: Franco-Colombo.

Rinehart & Company, Inc., 232 Madison Avenue, New York 16, N.Y,

Rudolf M. Rohrer Verlag, Kohlmarkt 7, Vienna 1, Austria.

The Roundelay Corporation of America, 416 West Briar Place, Chicago 14, Illinois.

Royal Musical Association, Dr. Nigel Fortune, Secretary, 44 Philip Victor Road, Handsworth, Birmingham, England.

Royal School of Church Music, Addington Palace, Croyden, Surrey, England.

Rufer-Verlag, Eickhoffstr. 12, Gütersloh, Germany.

SCS. Agent: Artia.

SHV. See Státní Hudební Vydavatelství.

SNKL. See Státní Nakladatelství Krásné Literatury a Umění.

SNKLHU. Agent: Artia.

SPN. Agent: Artia.

SVKL. See Slovenské Vydavatelstvo Krásnej Literatúry.

Mário de Sampayo Ribeiro, rua Viriato 6-III-D, Lisbon 1, Portugal.

Casa Editrice Sansoni, Viale Mazzini 46, Florence. Order from Libreria Commissionaria Sansoni, Export Department, via Gino Capponi 26, Florence, Italy.

Sanssouci-Verlag, Rosenbühlstr. 37, Zurich, Switzerland.

G. Schirmer, Inc., 609 Fifth Avenue, New York 17, N.Y.

Musikantiquariat Hans Schneider, Mozart-Weg 1, Tutzing über München, Germany.

B. Schott's Söhne Musikverlag, Postfach 1403, Weihergarten, 5, 6500 Mainz, Germany. U.S.: AMP.

Schulmerich Electronics, Sellersville, Pennsylvania. No publications available.

Editrice La Scuola, via Luigi Cadorna 11, Brescia, Italy.

Scuola Tipografica Benedettina, Parma. Benedettini di S.
　Giovanni (Tipografia), 1, pl. s. Giovanni, Parma, Italy?
Éditions Seghers, 228 Boulevard Raspail, Paris 14, France.
Éditions du Seuil, 27, rue Jacob, Paris 6, France.
Musikverlag Hans Sikorski, Johnsallee 23, 2000 Hamburg
　13, Germany.
Slovenské Vydavatelstvo Krásnej Literatúry, Michalská ul.
　9, Bratislava, Czechoslovakia. Agent: Artia.
Sociedad Colombista Panamericana, L. Pérez 251, Havana,
　Cuba.
Società di Storia Patria per la Puglia, Bari, Italy.
Société Française de Diffusion Musicale et Artistique,
　22 rue L.-Bellan, Paris 2; also éditeur, 12 rue
　Croissant, Paris, France.
Société Française de Musicologie, 45 & 47, rue La Boétie,
　Paris 8, France. Agent: Heugel. U.S.: Presser.
South African Society of Music Teachers, c/o Mrs.
　M. E. de Graaf, Business Manager, St. Hellers Rouwkoop
　Road, Rondebosch, Capetown; also Head Office, 119
　Middle Str., Nieuw Muckleneuk, Pretoria, Union of
　South Africa.
Southern Music Publishing Company, Inc., 1619 Broadway,
　New York 19, N. Y.
Stainer & Bell, 29 Newman St., London W. 1, England.
Státní Hudební Vydavatelství, Nové Město, Palackého, ul.
　1, Prague, 1, Czech. Agent: Artia.
Státní Nakladatelství Krásné literatury a umění, Nové
　Město, Národní tř. 36, Prague 1, Czech. Agent:
　Artia.
Staufen-Verlag Paul Bercker, Postfach 29, Moerser Str.
　313, 4132 Kamp-Lintfort, Germany.
Summy-Birchard Company, 1834 Ridge Ave., Evanston,
　Illinois.
Summy Publishing Company. Agent: Summy-Birchard.
Tafelberg-Uitgewers Beperk, P. O. Box 879, 4 Wale St.,
　Capetown, Union of South Africa.

Libreria Ticci, Banchi di Sopra 52, Siena, Italy.

Alec Tiranti Ltd., 72 Charlotte St., London W. 1, England.

P. J. Tonger Musikverlag, Bergstr. 10, 5038 Rodenkirchen, Germany.

Edition Tonos, Tonos Verlag Franz König, Aha Str. 7, 6100 Darmstadt 2, Germany.

De Torentrans, Lijnmarkt 43, Utrecht, Holland.

Konrad Triltsch, Haugerring 15/19, Würzburg, Germany.

Tsentr, K-T na DKMS, Otd. "Propaganda i agitatsiîa,"
Sofia, Bulgaria.

UNESCO, place de Fontenoy, Paris 7, France.

Universal-Edition, Karlsplatz 6, Vienna 1, Austria. U. S. : Presser.

Universidad Catolica de Chile, Facultad de Ciencias y Artes Musicales, O'Higgins 245, Santiago de Chile, Chile.

Universitätsverlag Freiburg, Pérolles 39, Fribourg, Switzerland.

Universitetsbiblioteket i Oslo, Drammensveien 42b, Oslo, Norway.

Universitetsforlaget, Karl Johansgt. 47, Oslo, Norway.

University of California Library, Berkeley 4, California.
Music Library Manuals are not available.

University of California Press, Berkeley 4, California.

Éditions du Vieux Colombier. See La Colombe.

Voggenreiter Verlag, Meckenheimer Str. 12, 5320 Bad Godesberg-Mehlem, Germany.

Arno Volk-Verlag, Drususgasse 7/11, 5000 Cologne, Germany.

Volk und Wissen Volkseigener Verlag, Lindenstr. 54a, Berlin W. 8, GDR.

Walsh, Holmes & Co. Ltd., 148 Charing Cross Road, London W. C. 2, England.

Otto Walter-Verlag, Amthausquai 21, Olten/Solothurn, Switzerland.

Willi Webels Verlagsbuchhandlung, Bochumer Str. 55,

4300 Essen-Steele, Germany.

Bühnen-und Musikalienverlag Joseph Weinberger, Mahlerstr. 11, Vienna 1, Austria.

Westfälische Landeskirchenmusikschule, Parkstr. 6, Herford, Germany.

Yale School of Music, Yale University, New Haven, Connecticut.

Yale University Press, 92A Yale Station, New Haven, Connecticut.

Zeneműkiadó Vállalat, Semmelweis ütca 1-3, Budapest 5, Hungary. Agent: Kultura.

Zwingli Verlag, Cramerstr. 17, Zurich, Switzerland.

Index to Series and Issuing Organizations

Archives of Recorded Music. See Archives de la musique enregistrée.

Argumente; eine Schriftenreihe für den Harmonika-Lehrer (Harmonikalehrer)

Association Internationale des Bibliothèques Musicales. See (1) Catalogus musicus; (2) Conseil International de la Musique; (3) Documenta musicologica.

Association Saint Ambroise Pour le Chant Sacré du Peuple. See Kinnor.

Associazione Italiana Santa Cecilia. See Biblioteca di cultura ceciliana.

Bach-Archiv, Leipzig. See (1) Bach-Dokumente; (2) Faksimile-Reihe Bachscher Werke und Schriftstücke.

Bach-Dokumente (Bärenreiter)

Bach-Studien (Breitkopf & Härtel)

Basilienses de musica orationes (Bärenreiter)

Bausteine für Musikerziehung und Musikpflege (Schott)

Beethovenhaus, Bonn. See Veröffentlichungen des Beethovenhauses.

Beiträge zur Gegenwartsfragen der Musik (Hohler)

Beiträge zur Geschichte des Alt-Wiener Musikverlages (Universal et al)

Beiträge zur mittelrheinischen Musikgeschichte (Schott et al)

Beiträge zur Musikerziehung (Merseburger)

Beiträge zur rheinischen Musikgeschichte (Volk et al)

Beiträge zur Schulmusik (Möseler). *Martens-Münnich; Beiträge zur Schulmusik.

Beiträge zur steirischen Musikforschung. See Musik aus der Steiermark.

Belgische Vereeniging voor Muziekwetenschap. See Publications de la Société Belge de Musicologie.

Berliner Studien zur Musikwissenschaft (Merseburger)

Berner Veröffentlichungen zur Musikforschung (P. Haupt)

Beroemde musici (Kruseman)

Bibliografia polskich czasopism muzycznych (PWM)

Biblioteca degli "Historiae musicae cultores." See "Historiae musicae cultores" biblioteca.

Biblioteca di cultura ceciliana (Associazione Italiana Santa Cecilia)

Biblioteca di cultura musicale (Guanda)

Biblioteca sansoniana musicale (Sansoni)

Biblioteka Chopinowska (PWM)

Biblioteka "Muzikalno, teatralno, i izobrazitelno izkustva" (Tsentr. K-T na DKMS)

Biblioteka Państwowej Wyzszej Szkoły Muzycznej. See Państwowa Wyższa Szkoła Muzyczna.

Biblioteka słuchacza koncertowego (PWM)

Bibliotheca musica (Zeneműkiadó Vállalat)

Bibliotheca musicae (Istituto Editoriale Italiano)

Bibliothèque de la Faculté de philosophie et lettres de l'Université de Liége. See Colloques.

Black Bull Chapbooks (Rams Skull)

Bonn. See Veröffentlichungen des Beethovenhauses.

Brünn. Universita. See (1) Hudební knihovna Rovnosti; (2) Janáčkův archiv; (3) Práce ze Semináře.

Bŭlgarska Akademiïă na Naukite. Trudove na Instituta za Muzika (Bŭlgarska Akad.)

Les Cahiers du Journal Musical Français (Société Française de Diffusion Musicale)

California. (See (1) Music Library Manuals; (2) University of California Publications in Music.

Catalogue des oeuvres de compositeurs belges (Centre Belge de Documentation Musicale)

Catalogue of Works by Members of the Composers' Guild of Great Britain (Composers' Guild)

Catalogus musicus (Internationale Vereinigung der Musikbibliotheken) *International Association of Music Libraries. Catalogus musicus. musicus.

Catholic University of America Studies in Music (Catholic University of America Press)

Centre Belge de Documentation Musicale. See Catalogue des oeuvres de compositeurs belges.

Centro de Estudios Folclóricos y Musicales, Bogotá. See Monografías del Centro.

Centro di Studi Palestriniani. See Collana di Studi Palestriniani.

Cercle International d'Études Ethno-Musicologiques. See Colloques de Wégimont.

Chile. See Universidad de Chile.

The Choirmaster's Notebook Series (Fortress Press)

Church Music Society. Occasional Papers (Oxford University Press)

----. Shorter Papers (Oxford University Press)

The Church Musician 's Bookshelf (Gregorian Institute of America)

Colección de ensayos. See Universidad de Chile.

Colección Labor (Labor)

Collana di "Musica jazz" (Messaggerie Musicali)

Collana di Studi Palestriniani (Centro di Studi Palestriniani)

Collectanea historiae musicae. See "Historiae musicae cultores" biblioteca.

Collection des biographies pratiques à l'usage des étudiants en musique (Lire)

Collection d'études musicologiques; Sammlung musikwissenschaftlicher Abhandlungen (Heitz). *Sammlung musikwissenschaftlicher Abhandlungen.

Collection Euterpe (Colombe)

Collection "Les documents célèbres" (Cervin)

Collection Triptyque (Masse)

Collections Microcosme. See Solfèges.

Collezione "Euterpe" (Faro)

Collezione "Letteratura musicale" (Feltrinelli). *Letteratura musicale.

Les colloques de Wégimont. Ethnomusicologie (Various).

Colombia. See Monografías del Centro.

Columbia University Studies in Musicology (Columbia Univ.

Press)

Commission Internationale des Arts et Traditions Populaires.
See Archives de la musique enregistrée, Série C.

The Commonwealth and International Library of Science,
Technology, Engineering and Liberal Studies. Music
Division (Macmillan).

Componisten-Serie (Gottmer)

Composer's Guild of Great Britain. See Catalogue of Works.

Los Compositores de música (Sociedad Colombista Panamericana)

Conseil International de la Musique. Répertoires internationaux de musique contemporaine à l'usage des amateurs
et des jeunes (Peters).

----. See also International Music Council. Publications.

Consejo Superior de Investigaciones Científicas. Instituto
Español de Musicología. Monografías (C. S. I. C.)

Corpus scriptorum de musica (American Institute of Musicology)

Čtení o hudbě (Panton)

Darmstadt. See Veröffentlichungen des Instituts für Neue
Musik und Musikerziehung.

Decca Music Guides (Cassell)

Detroit Studies in Music Bibliography (Information Service)

Deutscher Musikrat. See Musikalische Zeitfragen.

Deutsches Pädagogisches Zentralinstitut. See Methodische
Beiträge zum Unterricht im Fach Musik.

Dirección General de Relaciones Culturales. See Música en
Compostela.

Documenta musicologica (Bärenreiter)

Documents sur la musique (Massé)

Drucke zur Münchner Musikgeschichte (Ricke). *Münchner
Musikgeschichte. Drucke.

Edícia hudobnej literatúry (SHV et al)

Erlanger Arbeiten zur Musikwissenschaft (Ricke)

Ethno-Musicologica (Brill)

Ethnomusicologie. See Colloques de Wégimont.

Évocations des Jeunesses Musicales de Belgique (Jeunesses Musicales). *Jeunesses Musicales de Belgique. Évocations.

Fachbuchreihe Das Musikinstrument (Das Musikinstrument)

Facsimile Reprints. See Hinrichsen's Facsimile Reprints.

Faksimile-Reihe Bachscher Werke und Schriftstücke (Bärenreiter)

The Field of Music (Rinehart)

Folkeuniversitetets Bibliotek; Musik (Rhodos)

Folkeuniversitetsforeningen i København. See Folkeuniversitetets Bibliotek.

Fonds Daniele Cohen-Deswarte. See Catalogue des oeuvres de compositeurs belges.

Forschungsbeiträge zur Musikwissenschaft (Bosse)

Fountain Music Series (Fountain)

Freiburger Studien zur Musikwissenschaft (Universitätsverlag et al). *Fribourg. Université. Musikwissenschaftliches Institut. Veröffentlichungen.

Freie Universität Berlin. See Berliner Studien zur Musikwissenschaft.

Fribourg. See Freiburger Studien zur Musikwiss.

Gesellschaft der Orgelfreunde. See Veröffentlichungen der Gesellschaft der Orgelfreunde.

Gesellschaft für Musikforschung. See Musikwissenschaftliche Arbeiten.

Gesellschaft zur Förderung der Systematischen Musikwissenschaft. See Orpheus.

Göttinger musikwissenschaftliche Arbeiten (Bärenreiter)

Gottmer muziek pockets (Gottmer)

I Grandi musicisti (Guanda)

Les Grands compositeurs du XXe siècle (Kister)

Les Grands musiciens (Coudrier)

Gregorian Institute of America. See Church Musician's Bookshelf.

Die grossen Komponisten des 20. Jahrhunderts (Kister)

Guide musicali (Fussi)

Guide musicali dell'Istituto d'Alta Cultura (Istituto).
    *Istituto d'Alta Cultura, Milan. Guide musicali.

Hamburger Telemann-Gesellschaft. See Veröffentlichungen
    der Hamburger Telemann-Gesellschaft.

Herford. See Schriftenreihe der Westfälischen Landes-
    kirchenmusikschule.

Hesses Handbücher der Musik (Hesse)

Hesses kleine Bücherei (Hesse)

Hinrichsen's Facsimile Reprints (Hinrichsen)

Hinrichsen's Miniature Surveys (Hinrichsen)

"Historiae musicae cultores" biblioteca (Olschki). *Biblio-
    teca degli "Historiae musicae cultores."

Hudba na každém kroku (SHV)

Hudebně-pedagogická knihovna Rovnosti (Rovnost)

Hudební Edice SSÚ (Krajské nakl. / Ostrava). *Opava,
    Czech. Slezský studijní ústav.

Hudební knihovna Rovnosti (Rovnost). *Rovnost, Brünn.
    Hudební knihovna.

Hudební příručky pro každého (Pazdírkovo Nakl. Brno)

Hudební profily (SHV et al)

Hudební rozpravy (SHV et al)

Hudobné profily (SHV)

Hymn Society of America. See Papers of the Hymn Society
    of America.

Institut für Musikforschung, Regensburg. See (1) Archives
    de la musique enregistrée, Série C; (2) Quellen und
    Forschungen zur musikalischen Folklore.

Institut für Neue Musik und Musikerziehung, Darmstadt.
    See Veröffentlichungen des Institutes.

Institute of Mediaeval Music, Brooklyn. See (1) Musical
    Theorists in Translation; (2) Musicological Studies.

Instituto d'Alta Cultura, Milan. See Guide musicali dell'
    Istituto.

Instituto de Investigaciones Musicales. See Universidad de Chile.

Instituto Español de Musicología. See Consejo Superior de Investigaciones Científicas.

Institutt for Musikkvitenskap, Universitet i Oslo. Skrifter (Universitetsforlaget & H. Lyche). *Oslo. Universitet. Institutt for Musikkvitenskap. Skrifter.

Instituut voor Musiekwetenschap der Rijksuniversiteit te Utrecht. See Utrechtse bijdragen.

International Association of Music Libraries. See (1) Catalogus musicus; (2) Conseil International de la Musique; (3) Documenta musicologica.

International Commission on Folk Arts and Folklore. See Archives de la musique enregistrée, Série C.

International Folk Music Council. See Archives de la musique enregistrée, Série C.

International Music Council. Publications (UNESCO).

----. See also Conseil International de la Musique.

International Musicological Society. See (1) Catalogus musicus; (2) Documenta musicologica.

Internationale Gesellschaft für Musikwissenschaft. See (1) Catalogus musicus; (2) Documenta musicologica.

Internationale Vereinigung der Musikbibliotheken. See (1) Catalogus musicus; (2) Conseil International de la Musique; (3) Documenta musicologica.

Internationaler Musikrat. See (1) Conseil International de la Musique; (2) International Music Council; (3) Deutscher Musikrat.

Janáčkův archiv (SNKLHM et al)

Jazz (Hörsta)

Jazz Bücherei (Pegasus)

Jazz Monographs (Allen)

Jazz Publications (Jazz Publications)

Jenaer Beiträge zur Musikforschung (Breitkopf & Härtel)

Jeunesses Musicales de Belgique. See Évocations des Jeunesses Musicales.

Journal Musical Français. See Cahiers du Journal Musical
  Français.
Kantelenreeks (Torentrans)
Katowice, Poland. See Państwowa Wyższa Szkoła Muzyczna.
Keystone Books in Music (Lippincott)
Kiel. See Schriften des Landesinstituts für Musikforschung.
Kieler Schriften zur Musikwissenschaft. See Schriften des
  Landesinstituts für Musikforschung.
Kings of Jazz (Cassell)
Kings of Jazz (Niggli)
Kinnor (Fleurus)
Kis zenei könyvtár (Gondolat)
Klasikové hudební vĕdy a kritiky (SHV et al)
Kleine Bücherei des Harmonika-Freundes (Hohner)
Kleine Jazz-Bibliothek (Papillons)
Das kleine Musikbuch (Tonos)
Kleine Musikbücherei (Sikorski)
Knihovna klasiků. Musikologické spisy (SNKL).
Knižnice Hudebních rozhledů (Panton)
Kölner Beiträge zur Musikforschung (Bosse)
Kommission für Musikforschung, Vienna. See (1) Mitteilun-
  gen der Kommission; (2) Veröffentlichungen der Kommis-
  sion.
Kommission für Musikwissenschaft der Akademie der Wis-
  senschaften und der Literatur. See Neue Studien zur
  Musikwissenschaft.
Kontrapunkte; Schriften zur Deutschen Musik der Gegenwart
  (Tonger)
Künstler der Schallplatte (Bielefelder)
Kurze Biographien grosser Komponisten (Daisan Shobô)
Kustannustalon musiikkiopas (Kustannustalo)
Leren luisteren (Nederlandsche Boekhandel)
Letteratura musicale. See Collezione "Letteratura musicale."
Literarhistorisch-musikwissenschaftliche Abhandlungen
  (Triltsch)
Magyar zenetudomány (Zeneműkiadó Vállalat)

Les Maîtres du jazz (Belvédère)
Maɫa biblioteka operowa (PWM)
Male monografie muzyczne (PWM)
Man and His Music (Oxford et al)
Martens-Münnich; Beiträge zur Schulmusik. See Beiträge
   zur Schulmusik.
Materiaɫy do bibliografii muzyki polskiej (PWM)
Max-Reger-Institut, Bonn. See Veröffentlichungen des Max-
   Reger-Institutes.
Meister der leichten Musik (Amalthea)
Meister der Operette (Amalthea)
Merlin Music Books (Merlin)
Methodische Beiträge zum Unterricht im Fach Musik
   (Volk und Wissen Volkseigener Verlag). *Germany (Dem-
   ocratic Republic, 1949-). Deutsches Pädagogisches
   Zentralinstitut. Sektion Unterrichtsmethodik und Lehr-
   pläne. Methodische Beiträge zum Unterricht im Fach
   Musik.
Miniature Surveys. See Hinrichsen's Miniature Surveys.
Ministerium für Kultur. See Studienmaterial.
Miscellanea (Miscellaneous). See American Institute of
   Musicology.
Mitteilungen der Kommission für Musikforschung (Rohrer).
   *Akademie der Wissenschaften, Vienna. Kommission
   für Musikforschung. Mitteilungen.
Monografías. See Consejo Superior de Investigaciones
   Científicas.
Monografías del Centro de Estudios Folclóricos y Musicales
   (Centro)
Monographs in Theory and Composition (Music Teachers
   National Association)
Monographs on the Art of Piano Teaching (Walsh, Holmes)
Montevideo. See Museo Histórico Nacional.
Moravian Music Foundation Publications (Moravian Music
   Foundation)
Münchner Musikgeschichte. See Drucke zur Münchner

Musikgeschichte.

Münchner Veröffentlichungen zur Musikgeschichte (Schneider)

Museo Histórico Nacional. Sección de Musicología (Museo).

*Montevideo. Museo Histórico Nacional. Sección de Musicología. Publicación.

Music From the Belfry (Schulmerich)

Music Library Manuals (Univ. of Calif. Library). *California. University. Library. Music Library Manuals.

Music Teachers National Association. See Monographs in Theory and Composition.

Music Theory Translation Series (Yale School of Music)

Musica d'oggi. See Quaderni di "Musica d'oggi."

Música en Compostela (Dirección General de Relaciones Culturales)

La Musica moderna (Balcone)

Musical Theorists in Translation (Institute of Mediaeval Music)

Musica-Serie; kleine boeken over grote mannen (Kruseman)

Musices graecai corrigenda (Dabo-Peranić)

Musiche e musicisti pugliesi (Società di Storia Patria)

Musiciens de tous les temps (Seghers)

Musiciens et leurs oeuvres (Rouge)

Musicisti della nostra terra (Drago)

Musicisti italiani dell'800 (Athena)

Musicologica (Brill)

Musicologica medii aevi (Noord-Hollandsche)

Musicological Studies; Wissenschaftliche Abhandlungen (Institute of Mediaeval Music). *Institute of Mediaeval Music, Brooklyn. Musicological Studies.

Musicological Studies and Documents (Amer. Institute of Musicology). *American Institute of Musicology. Musicological Studies and Documents.

Musiekbiblioteek (Tafelberg)

Musik aus der Steiermark (Akademische)

Musik der Zeit; eine Schriftenreihe zu Musik und Gegenwart
 (Boosey & Hawkes)
Musik der Zeit; eine Schriftenreihe zur zeitgenössischen
 Musik (Boosey & Hawkes)
Die Musik im alten und neuen Europa (Hinnenthal)
Musik und Zeit (Mitteldeutscher Verlag)
Musikalische Gegenwartsfragen (Müller-Thiergarten)
Musikalische Zeitfragen (Bärenreiter)
Musikalisches Brevier (Hinnenthal)
Musikaliska Akademien, Stockholm. See Publikationer utg.
 av Kungl. Musikaliska Akademien med Musikhögskolan.
Musikaliska Akademien, Stockholm. Bibliotek. See
 Publikationer utg. av Kungl. Musikaliska Akademiens
 Biblioteket
Musik-bibliotek (Hansen)
Musikbücherei für jedermann (Breitkopf & Härtel)
Musiker, die der Welt gehören (Weinberger)
Musiker-Portraits. See Pechan-Reihe; Musiker-Portraits.
Musikerreihe (Walter)
Der Musikfreund (Kaltschmid)
Das Musikinstrument. See (1) Fachbuchreihe Das Musikin-
 strument; (2) Schriftenreihe Das Musikinstrument.
Musiknovellen (Crüwell)
Musikpädagogische Bibliothek (Quelle & Meyer)
Musikschulwerk (Hofmeister)
Musikwissenschaft (Mondial)
Musikwissenschaftliche Arbeiten (Bärenreiter)
Musikwissenschaftliche Einzeldarstellungen (Breitkopf &
 Härtel)
Musikwissenschaftliche Reihe im Voggenreiter Verlag
 (Voggenreiter)
Musikwissenschaftliche Studienbibliothek (Gennrich)
De Muziek (Kruseman)
Muziek-paedogogische bibliotheek (Muusses)
Muzikološki Institut, Srpska Akademija Nauka. See
 Srpska Akademija Nauka.

National School Brass Band Association Handbooks (Hinrichsen)

Neue Studien zur Musikwissenschaft (Schott). *Akademie der Wissenschaften und der Literatur, Mainz. Kommission für Musikwissenschaft. Neue Studien zur Musikwissenschaft.

Neujahrsblatt der Allgemeinen Musikgesellschaft Zürich (Hug)

Novello's Music Primers (Novello)

Nueva visión; música (Neuva Visión)

Occasional Papers. See Church Music Society.

Oesterreichische Akademie der Wissenschaften. See (1) Mitteilungen der Kommission für Musikforschung; (2) Veröffentlichungen der Kommission für Musikforschung.

Opava, Czech. See Hudební edice SSÚ.

Opera Pocket Books (Black)

Operní libreta Antonína Dvořáka (SNKLHU)

Organik (Möseler)

Orgel-Monographien (Rheingold)

Orgelwissenschaftliche Arbeits- und Musikgemeinschaft. Rundbrief (R. Haupt)

Orgues d'Alsace (Europea)

Orpheus-Bücher (Hollinek)

Orpheus; Schriftenreihe zu Grundfragen der Musik (Gesellschaft zur Förderung der Systematischen Musikwissenschaft)

Oslo. See Institutt for Musikkvitenskap, Universitet i Oslo.

Pamfletreeks. See Pamphlet Series.

Pamphlet Series; Pamfletreeks (South African Society of Music Teachers). *South African Society of Music Teachers. Pamphlet Series.

Pan American Music Series (Southern). *Pan American Union. Division of Music and Visual Arts. Music Series.

Panśtwowa Wyższa Szkoła Muzyczna w Katowicach. Biblioteka. Katalogi.

----. Biblioteka. Prace Biblioteki. *Katowice, Poland.
Państwowa Wyższa Szkoła Muzyczna. Biblioteka. Prace
Biblioteki.

----. Biblioteka. Wykłady i prelekcje.

----. Lektorat języka niemieckiego. Przekłady.

Papers of the Hymn Society of America (Hymn Society).
*Hymn Society of America. Papers.

Pechan-Reihe; Musiker-Portraits (Pechan)

Phoenix Music Guides (Phoenix House)

Piccola biblioteca Ricordi (Ricordi)

Posebna Izdanja. See Srpska Akademija Nauka.

Pour la musique (Gallimard)

Prace Biblioteki. See Państwowa Wyższa Szoła Muzyczna.

Práce ze Semináře hudební výchovy na Masarykově Uni-
versitě v Brně (Hudební Matice). *Brünn. Universita.
Seminář hudební výchovy. Práce.

Publications. See International Music Council.

Publications de la Société Belge de Musicologie;
Uitgaven van de Belgische Vereeniging voor Muziekwe-
tenschap (Nederlandsche Boekhandel). *Société Belge de
Musicologie. Publications.

Publications de la Société Française de Musicologie (Heugel).
*Société Française de Musicologie. Publications.

Publications of the Library of the Royal Swedish Academy
of Music. See Publikationer utg. av Kungl. Musikaliska
Akademiens Biblioteket.

Publikationen der Schweizerischen Musikforschenden
Gesellschaft (P. Haupt). *Schweizerische Musikforschende
Gesellschaft. Publikationen.

Publikationer utg. av Kungl. Musikaliska Akademien med
Musikhögskolan (Nordiska). *Kungl. Musikaliska Akademien, Stockholm. Publikationer.

Publikationer utg. av Kungl. Musikaliska Akademiens
Biblioteket; Publications of the Library of the Royal
Swedish Academy of Music (Musikaliska Akademiens Bib-
lioteket). *Kungl. Musikaliska Akademien, Stockholm.

Bibliotek.   Publikationer.

Quaderni dell'Accademia Musicale Chigiana (Ticci). *Siena.
Accademia Musicale Chigiana. Quaderni.

Quaderni di "Musica d'oggi" (Ricordi)

Quaderni di "Vita nuova" (Scuola Tip. Benedettina)

Quellen und Forschungen zur musikalischen Folklore (Bosse)

Quellenhefte zur Musikkunde und Musikgeschichte im Schul-
unterricht (Crüwell)

R. M. A. Research Chronicle (Royal Musical Asso.)

Record Collector's Series (E. M. I.)

Record Handbook (Allen)

Régi magyar dallamok tára (Akadémiai Kiadô)

Die Reihe; Information über serielle Musik (Universal;
Eng. ed.: Presser)

Répertoires internationaux de musique. See Conseil International de la Musique.

Rijksuniversiteit te Utrecht. See Utrechtse bijdragen.

Rovnost, Brünn. See Hudební knihovny Rovnosti.

Royal Musical Association. See R. M. A.

Royal School of Church Music. Study Notes (Royal School)

Rundbrief. See Orgelwissenschaftliche Arbeits- und
Musikgemeinschaft.

Rural Music Schools Association. See Fountain Music Series.

Saggi di storia e letteratura musicale (Genio)

Sammlung musikwissenschaftlicher Abhandlungen. See
Collection d'études musicologiques.

Sammlung musikwissenschaftlicher Einzeldarstellungen
(Breitkopf & Härtel)

Sanssouci-Jazz-Bibliothek (Sanssouci)

School of Bach-Playing for the Organist (Hinrichsen)

Schriften des Landesinstituts für Musikforschung, Kiel
(Bärenreiter). *Kiel. Landesinstitut für Musikforschung.
Schriften.

Schriftenreihe Das Musikinstrument (Musikinstrument)

Schriftenreihe der Westfälischen Landeskirchenmusikschule
in Herford (Rufer). *Herford, Germany. Westfälische

Landeskirche. Schriftenreihe.

Schriftenreihe des Allgemeinen Cäcilien-Verbandes für die Länder der deutschen Sprache (Herder)

Schriftenreihe des Schweizerischen Arbeitskreises für Kirchenmusik (Zwingli)

Schweizerische Musikforschende Gesellschaft. See Publikationen der Schweizerischen Musikforschenden Gesellschaft.

Schweizerischer Arbeitskreis für Kirchenmusik. See Schriftenreihe des Schweizerischen Arbeitskreises für Kirchenmusik.

Shorter Papers. See Church Music Society.

Siena. See Quaderni dell'Accademia Musicale Chigiana.

I Signori dell'armonia (Palatine)

Skrifter. See Institutt for Musikkvitenskap, Universitetet i Oslo.

Sociedad Colombista Panamericana. See Los Compositores de Música.

Società di Storia Patria per la Puglia. See Musiche e musicisti pugliesi.

Société Belge de Musicologie. See Publications de la Société Belge de Musicologie.

Société Française de Diffusion Musicale et Artistique. See Cahiers du Journal Musical Française.

Société Française de Musicologie. See Publications de la Société Française de Musicologie.

Société Internationale de Musicologie. See International Musicological Society.

Solfèges (Seuil)

Sonatine-reeks (Nederland's Boekhuis)

South African Society of Music Teachers. See Pamphlet Series.

Spisy Janáčkovy akademie muzických umění (SPN)

Srpska Akademija Nauka. Posebna Izdanja. Muzikološki Institut (Naucna Knjiga).

Star-Galerie (Neuzeit)

Stimmen des **XX.** Jahrhunderts (Hesse)

Storia della musica (Bocca)

Studia i materiały do dziejów muzyki polskiej (PWM)

Studia musicologica upsaliensia (Almqvist & Wiksell)

Studienmaterial für die künstlerischen Lehranstalten der
Deutschen Demokratischen Republik (Verlag der Kunst)

Studies and Documents. See American Musicological Society.
Studies and Documents.

Studies in Music. See Catholic Univ. of America.

Study Notes. See Royal School of Church Music.

Suid-Afrikaanse Vereniging van Musiekonderwysers. See
Pamphlet Series.

Summa musicae medii aevi (Gennrich)

Summy Piano Teaching Pamphlet Series (Summy)

Symposium (Ricordi)

Trudove na Instituta za Muzika. See Bŭlgarska Akademiiā na
Naukite.

Tübinger Bach-Studien (Hohner)

Uitgaven van de Belgische Vereeniging voor Muziekwetenschap. See Publications de la Sociêtê Belge de
Musicologie.

UNESCO. See Archives de la musique enregistrée.

Universidad de Chile, Instituto de Investigaciones Musicales,
Facultad de Ciencias y Artes Musicales. Colección de
ensayos. *Chile. Universidad, Santiago. Instituto de Investigaciones Musicales. Colección de ensayos.

Universidad Nacional de Colombia. See Monografías del
Centro.

Universität Freiburg in der Schweiz. See Freiburger
Studien zur Musikwissenschaft.

Universitet i Oslo. See Institutt for Musikkvitenskap.

University of California Library. See Music Library
Manuals.

University of California Publications in Music (Univ. of
Calif. Press).   *California. University. University of
California Publications in Music.

Utrechtse bijdragen tot de muziekwetenschap (Creyghton)
Veröffentlichungen der Gesellschaft der Orgelfreunde
(various). *Gesellschaft der Orgelfreunde. Veröffent-
lichungen.
Veröffentlichungen der Hamburger Telemann-Gesellschaft
(Sikorski). *Hamburger Telemann-Gesellschaft. Veröffent-
lichungen.
Veröffentlichungen der Kommission für Musikforschung
(Böhlau). *Akademie der Wissenschaften, Vienna. Kom-
mission für Musikforschung. Veröffentlichungen.
Veröffentlichungen des Beethovenhauses in Bonn (Beethoven-
Haus). *Bonn. Beethovenhaus. Veröffentlichungen.
Veröffentlichungen des Instituts für Neue Musik und Musiker-
ziehung Darmstadt (Merseburger). *Darmstadt. Institut
für Neue Musik und Musikerziehung. Veröffentlichungen.
Veröffentlichungen des Max-Reger-Institutes, Elsa-Reger-
Stiftung, Bonn (Dümmler). *Max-Reger-Institut, Bonn.
Veröffentlichungen.
Veröffentlichungen des Musikwissenschaftlichen Instituts der
Freien Universität Berlin. See Berliner Studien zur
Musikwissenschaft.
Vita nuova. See Quaderni di "Vita nuova."
Voices of the Past; A Catalogue of Vocal Recordings (Oak-
wood)
Westfälische Landeskirchenmusikschule in Herford. See
Schriftenreihe der Westfälische Landeskirchenmusikschule
in Herford.
Wiener Abhandlungen zur Musikwissenschaft und Instrument-
enkunde (Geyer)
Wiener Musik-Bücherei (Doblinger)
Wiener musikiwissenschaftliche Beiträge (Böhlau)
Wir fangen an (Hofmeister)
Wissenschaftliche Abhandlungen. See Musicological Studies;
Wissenschaftliche Abhandlungen.
The World of Music (Parrish; Chanticleer)
Wykłady i prelekcje. See Państwowa Wyższa Szkoła

Muzyczna.

Yale School of Music. See Music Theory Translation Series.

Yale Studies in the History of Music (Yale Univ. Press)

Young Reader's Guide to Music (Oxford Univ. Press)

Za novou hudbu (Orbis)

Zenetudományi tanulmányok (Akadémiai Kiadó)

Zródła pamiętnikarsko-literackie do dziejów muzyki polskiej (PWM)

Bibliography

Abhandlungen zur Kunst- , Musik- und Literaturwissenschaft
Bonn: Bouvier
1. Haas, H. Ueber die Bedeutung der Harmonik in den
   Liedern Franz Schuberts; zugleich ein Beitrag zur Methodik der harmonischen Analyse. 1957.
Vols. 2-11 do not concern music.
12. Riedel, H. Die Darstellung von Musik und Musikerlebnis
   in der erzählenden deutschen Dichtung. 1959. 2. durchges. Auflage 1961.
Vols. 13-17 do not concern music.
18. Ehrenforth, K. H.   Ausdruck und Form;
   Schönbergs Durchbruch zur Atonalität in den George-
   Liedern, op. 15. 1963.

Achegas para a história da música em Portugal
Lisboa (No. 5 in Coimbra): The Author
1. Sampayo Ribeiro, M. de.   A obra musical do Padre
   António Pereira de Figueiredo. 1932.
2. ----. Damião de Goes na Livraria Real de Música.
   1935.
3. ----. A música em Portugal nos séculos XVIII e XIX;
   bosquejo de história crítica. 1938.
4. ----. As "guitarras de Alcácer" e a "guitarra portu-
   guesa. " 1936.
5. ----. Os manuscritos musicais nos. 6 e 12 da Biblioteca
   Geral da Universidade de Coimbra; contribuição para um
   catálogo definitivo. 1941.
6. ----. Frei Manuel Cardoso; contribuição para o estudo
   da sua vida e da sua obra. 1961.

Achter de noten

Delft: W. Gaade
1. Nolthenius, H. Beethoven vanuit zijn muziek. 1956.
2. Loeser, N. Schuberts klankwereld. 1957.

Les Albums de la chanson
Monte-Carlo: Éditions de l'Heure
2. Macabiès, J. Johnny Hallyday. 1962.
3. Dictionnaire du rock, du twist et du madison en France. 1962.
5. Hiégel, P. Édith Piaf. 1962.

Amerbach-Musikbibliothek
Basel: Amerbach-Verlag
1. Refardt, E. Theodor Fröhlich; ein Schweizer Musiker der Romantik. 1947.
2. Tobler, E. Peter Jecklin; ein Kapitel aus Zürichs Musikleben. 1947.
3. Abraham, G. Ueber russische Musik. Ausgewählt und übers. von Willi Reich. 1947.

American Institute of Musicology. Miscellanea (= Miscellaneous).
Rome (No. 1); Nijmegen (No. 2): American Institute of Musicology. Partly music; partly numbered.
1. Le Jeune, C. Airs (1608). Ed. by D. P. Walker. Intro. by François Lesure & D. P. Walker. 4 vols. in 3. 1951-59.
2. Smits van Waesberghe, J. A Textbook of Melody; A Course in Functional Melodic Analysis. Trans. from the Dutch by W. A. G. Doyle-Davidson. 1955.

American Musicological Society. Studies and Documents.
New York: Galaxy (distributor). Partly numbered; partly music.
1. Ockeghem, J. de. Collected Works. Ed. by Dragan Plamenac. Vol. 2: Masses and Mass Sections IX-XVI. New York: Columbia Univ. Press, 1947. See No. 3 below.

2. Dunstable, J. Complete Works. Ed. by Manfred F.
Bukofzer. (=Musica Britannica, 8.) Published for the
Royal Musical Association and the American Musicologi-
cal Society. London: Stainer & Bell, 1953.
3. Ockeghem, J. de. Collected Works. Ed. by Dragan
Plamenac. Vol. 1: Masses I-VIII. 2nd corrected ed.
1959. 3rd ed. in prep. 1st ed.: Publikationen älterer
Musik, Jg. 1, Teil 2, Leipzig, 1927.
4. Kerman, J. The Elizabethan Madrigal; A Comparative
Study. 1962.
5. Aldrich, P. The Principal Agréments of the
Seventeenth and Eighteenth Centuries; A Study in Musical
Ornamentation. Harvard dissert. 1942. In prep. Exact
title unverified.

Arcadia-Starparade
Hamburg: Arcadia-Verlag, Sikorski
1. Schmacke, E. Friedel Hensch und die Cyprys. 1954.
2. ----. Vico Torriani. 1954.
3. ----. Bully Buhlan. 1954.
4. ----. Gerhard Wendland. 1954

Archives de la musique enregistrée; Archives of Recorded
Music
Paris: UNESCO (various publishers). Partly numbered.
Série A: Musique occidentale; Occidental Music
1. Panigel, A., et al. L'oeuvre de Frédéric Chopin;
discographie générale. Introduction et notes de Marcel
Beaufils. Paris: Revue Disques, 1949. French only.
2. L'oeuvre de J.S. Bach. Appearance unverified.
Série B: Musique orientale; Oriental Music
1. Daniélou, A. Catalogue de la musique indienne classique et traditionelle enregistrée; A Catalogue of Recorded
Classical and Traditional Indian Music. 1952. Fr. & Eng.
Série C: Musique ethnographique et folklorique; Ethnograph-
ical and Folk Music
1. Collection Phonothèque nationale (Paris). Catalogue

établi par la Commission internationale des arts et traditions populaires (C. I. A. P.); Catalogue prepared by the International Commission on Folk Arts and Folklore (CIAP). 1952. Fr. & Eng.

2. Collection Musée de l'homme (Paris). Catalogue établi [as above]. 1952. Fr. & Eng.
3. Katalog der europäischen Volksmusik im Schallarchiv des Instituts für Musikforschung Regensburg. Für die UNESCO zusammengestellt und herausgegeben durch das Institut für Musikforschung Regensburg. Redacteur: Felix Hoerburger. (=Quellen und Forschungen zur Musikalischen Folklore, 1). Regensburg: G. Bosse, 1952. German only.
4. International Catalogue of Recorded Folk Music; Catalogue international de la musique folklorique enregistrée. Prepared and published for UNESCO by The International Folk Music Council. Edited by Norman Fraser. Preface by R. Vaughan Williams; Intro. by Maud Karpeles. London: Oxford Univ. Press, 1954. Eng. & Fr. Ed. of 1953 in LC appears to be a pre-publication copy.

Argumente: eine Schriftenreihe für den Harmonikalehrer
Trossingen/Württ. : Verlag Der Harmonikalehrer
1. Haupt, R. Das Akkordeon in der Kirche. 1958.

Bach-Dokumente. Hrsg. vom Bach-Archiv, Leipzig, als Supplement zur Neuen Bach-Ausgabe.
Leipzig: Bach-Archiv (Bärenreiter)
1. Schriftstücke von der Hand Johann Sebastian Bachs. 1963?
2. Fremdschriftliche und gedruckte Dokumente zur Lebensgeschichte Johann Sebastian Bachs.
3. Bilddokumente zur Lebensgeschichte Johann Sebastian Bachs.

Bach-Studien
Leipzig: Breitkopf und Härtel

1. Werker, W. Studien über die Symmetrie im Bau der Fugen und die motivische Zusammengehörigkeit der Präludien und Fugen des "Wohltemperierten Klaviers" von Johann Sebastian Bach. 1922.
2. ----. Die Matthäus-Passion. 1923.
3. Neumann, W. J. S. Bachs Chorfuge; ein Beitrag zur Kompositionstechnik Bachs. 2. Auflage 1950. 3. Auflage 1953.
4. Dürr, A. Studien über die frühen Kantaten J. S. Bachs. 1951.

Basilienses de musica orationes. Hrsg. von L. Schrade. Basel: Bärenreiter
1. Wellesz, E. Die Hymnen der Ostkirche. 1962.

Bausteine für Musikerziehung und Musikpflege. Schriften-reihe. Hrsg. von Fritz Jöde.
Mainz: Verlag Junge Musik, Schott. Werkreihe (music) not included here.
1. Twittenhoff, W. Neue Musikschulen; eine Forderung unserer Zeit. 1951.
2. Kemper, J. Stimmpflege; eine Handwerkslehre im Grundriss. 1951.
3. Sambeth, H. M. Kinder bauen Musikinstrumente. Teil I: Gläserspiele, Holzspiele, Metallspiele, Schlagzeug. Mit Ergänzungsbogen. 1951.
4. Nitsche, P. Die Pflege der Kinderstimme; eine Anre-gung für alle, denen Kinder anvertraut sind. Band 1. 1951. Band 2: Praktischer Teil; Uebung am Lied (=Werk-reihe 120). 1954.
5. Wolschke, M. Der Weg zum Schul- und Jugendorchester; ein Arbeitsbuch. 1952.
6. Valentin, E. Kleine Bilder grosser Meister; ein musik-biographisches Lesebuch. 1951.
7. Schumann, H. Die Bambusflöte; eine Anleitung zur Herstellung verschiedener Flötentypen. 1952.
8. Twittenhoff, W. Jugend und Jazz; ein Beitrag zur Klärung. 1953.

9. Jöde, F. Das kann ich auch! Kleine Elementarlehre der Musik mit Singen, Instrumentenspiel und Tanz für Schule und Haus; Einführung in die "Musikantenfibel." 1953.

10. ----. Vom Wesen und Werden der Jugendmusik. 1954.

11. Erpf, H. R. Gegenwartskunde der Musik; Ideen, Kräfte, Ziele. 1954.

12. Twittenhoff, W. , & P. F. Scherber. Die Jugendmusikschule; Idee und Wirklichkeit. (=Neue Musikschulen, 2). 1956.

13. Stumme, W. Musikpflege und Musikerziehung in einer Landschaft. 1957.

14. Reusch, F. Sprechfibel für Kinder und Jugendliche. 1963.

Beiträge zu Gegenwartsfragen der Musik
Landsberg am Lech, Germany: Heinrich Hohler
1. Neumann, F. Tonalität und Atonalität; Versuch einer Klärung. 1955.
No more published.

Beiträge zur Geschichte des Alt-Wiener Musikverlages.
  Hrsg. von Alexander Weinmann.
Wien: Universal-Edition et al. Partly numbered.
Reihe 1: Komponisten
1. Weinmann, A. Verzeichnis der im Druck erschienenen Werke von Joseph Lanner, sowie Listen der Plattennummern der Originalausgaben für alle Besetzungen; ein bibliographischer Behelf. Leuen-Verlag (Krenn in Kommission), 1948.
2. ----. Verzeichnis sämtlicher Werke von Johann Strauss Vater und Sohn. Krenn, 1956.
Reihe 2: Verleger
1. ----. Verzeichnis der Verlagswerke des Musikalischen Magazins in Wien, 1784-1802, "Leopold Koželuch"; ein bibliographischer Behelf. Oesterreichischer Bundesverlag, 1950.

2. Weinmann, A. Vollständiges Verlagsverzeichnis Artaria & Comp. Krenn, 1952.

3. ----. Vollständiges Verlagsverzeichnis der Musikalien des Kunst- und Industrie Comptoirs in Wien, 1801-1819. In: Studien zur Musikwissenschaft, 22 (Wien: Oesterreichischer Bundesverlag, 1955), pp. 217-52.

4. ----. Verzeichnis der Musikalien des Verlages Johann Traeg in Wien, 1794-1818. In: Studien zur Musikwissenschaft, 23 (Wien: Oest. Bundesverlag, 1956), pp. 135-83.

5. ----. Wiener Musikverleger und Musikalienhändler von Mozarts Zeit bis gegen 1860; ein firmengeschichtlicher und topographischer Behelf. Rohrer in Kommission, 1956. (≑Oesterreichische Akademie der Wissenschaften, phil.-historische Klasse, Sitzungsberichte, 230. Band, 4. Abhandlung; also equals Veröffentlichungen der Kommission für Musikforschung, 2).

6. ----. Verzeichnis der Musikalien aus dem K.K. Hoftheater-Musik-Verlag. Universal-Edition, 1961.

7. ----. Kataloge Anton Huberty (Wien) und Christoph Torricella. Universal-Edition, 1962.

8. ----. Verlagsverzeichnis F.A. Hofmeister (Wien). In prep.

Beiträge zur mittelrheinischen Musikgeschichte
Mainz: Schott et al

1. Dunning, A.   Joseph Schmitt; Leben und Kompositionen des Eberbacher Zisterziensers und Amsterdamer Musikverlegers (1734-1791). Amsterdam: Heuwekemeyer, 1962.

2. Bösken, F. Die Orgeln der evangelischen Marienstiftskirche in Lich. Mainz: K. Schmidt in Kommission, 1962.

3. Gottron, A. Arnold Rucker, Orgelmacher von Seligenstadt. 1962.

4. Schmid, E.F. Die Orgeln von Amorbach; eine Musikgeschichte des Klosters. 2. Auflage, bearb. von Franz

Bösken. 1963.

Beiträge zur Musikerziehung
Berlin: Merseburger
1. Schmücker, E. Schule und musisches Leben. 1952. 3.
   Auflage 1961.
2. Tauscher, H. Praxis der rhythmisch-musikalischen
   Erziehung. 1952. 2. neu bearb. Auflage 1960.
3. Warner, T. Musische Erziehung zwischen Kult und
   Kunst. 1954.
4. Waldmann, G. Kleine Volksliedkunde. 1957.

Beiträge zur rheinischen Musikgeschichte. Hrsg. von der
   Arbeitsgemeinschaft für rheinische Musikgeschichte.
Köln: Staufen-Verlag, later Arno Volk (see also Nos. 7 &
   17)
1. Fellerer, K. G. , ed. Beiträge zur Musikgeschichte
   der Stadt Düsseldorf. Unter Mitarbeit von J. Alf, J.
   Loschelder, L. Schiedermair, F. Zobeley. 1952.
2. Eger von Kalkar, H. Cantuagium; eingeleitet und hrsg.
   von Heinrich Hüschen. 1952.
3. Kahl, W. Studien zur Kölner Musikgeschichte des 16.
   und 17. Jahrhunderts. 1953.
4. Lemacher, H. , ed. 125 Jahre Gürzenichchor Köln;
   Chronik der Jahre 1927-1952 zum 125jähr. Jubiläum des
   Gürzenichchores und der Kölner Concertgesellschaft.
   1953.
5. Fellerer, K. G. , ed. Beiträge zur Musikgeschichte
   der Stadt Wuppertal. Unter Mitarbeit von J. Alf, P.
   Greeff, W. Kahl, A. Krings, W. Reindell. 1954.
6. Brand, C. M. , & K. G. Fellerer, ed. Beiträge zur
   Musikgeschichte der Stadt Aachen. Unter Mitwirken von
   V. Aschoff, R. Haase, Th. B. Rehmann, J. Smits van
   Waesberghe, R. Zimmermann. 1954.
7. Wiora, W. Die rheinisch-bergischen Melodien bei
   Zuccalmaglio und Brahms; alte Liedweisen in romanti-
   scher Färbung. Bad Godesberg: Voggenreiter, 1953.

8. Fellerer, K. G., ed. Beiträge zur Musikgeschichte der Stadt Essen. Unter Mitarbeit von H. Eckert, W. Engelhardt, F. Feldens, R. Jahn, H. Kettering, K. Mews. 1955.

9. Bork, G. Die Melodien des Bonner Gesangbuches in seinen Ausgaben zwischen 1550 und 1630; eine Untersuchung über ihre Herkunft und Verbreitung. 1955.

10. Oepen, H. Beiträge zur Geschichte des Kölner Musiklebens, 1760-1840. 1955.

11. Wollick, N. Musica Gregoriana; Opus aureum, Köln 1501, pars I/II. Hrsg. von Klaus Wolfgang Niemöller. 1955. See also Heft 50.

12. Paffrath, H. Der Cäcilienverein 1855 Köln-Mülheim; ein Beitrag zur Mülheimer Musikgeschichte. 1955.

13. Niemöller, K. W. Nicolaus Wollick (1480-1541) und sein Musiktraktat. 1956.

14. Fellerer, K. G., ed. Beiträge zur Geschichte der Musik am Niederrhein. Unter Mitarbeit von K. Dreimüller, E. Klusen, C. Reuter, T. Zart. 1956.

15. Drux, H. Studien zur Entwicklung des öffentlichen Musiklebens in Ostniederberg. 1956.

16. Haase, R. Geschichte des Solinger Chorwesens. 1956.

17. Kettering, H. Quellen und Studien zur Essener Musikgeschichte des hohen Mittelalters. Essen: Webels, 1960.

18. Henseler, T. A. Max Reger und Bonn. 1957.

19. Brand, C. M., & K. G. Fellerer, ed. Musik im Rhein-Maas-Raum; Tagungsbericht Schleiden. Unter Mitarbeit von J. Alf, R. Haase, Hulverscheidt, H. Klotz, Quitin, J. Smits van Waesberghe, M. A. Vente. 1957.

20. Kahl, W., H. Lemacher, & J. Schmidt-Görg, ed. Studien zur Musikgeschichte des Rheinlandes; Festschrift zum 80. Geburtstag von Ludwig Schiedermair. 1956.

21. Neefe, C. G. Christian Gottlob Neefens Lebenslauf, von ihm selbst beschrieben. Nebst beigefügtem Karackter

1789. Eingeleitet und hrsg. von W. Engelhardt. 1957.

22. Smits van Waesberghe, J., ed. Herbeni Traiectensis De natura cantus ac miraculis vocis. 1957.

23. Niemöller, U. Carl Rosier (1640?-1725); Kölner Dom- und Ratskapellmeister. 1957.

24. Federhofer-Königs, R. Johannes Oridryus und sein Musiktraktat (Düsseldorf, 1557). 1957.

25. Schuh, P. Joseph Andreas Anschuez (1772-1855); der Gründer des Koblenzer Musikinstituts. 1958.

26. Fellerer, K.G., ed. Beiträge zur Musikgeschichte der Stadt Solingen und des Bergischen Lands. Unter Mitarbeit von Dreimüller, Haase, Lemacher, Paffrath, Schwermer. 1958.

27. Kahl, W. Katalog der in der Universitäts- und Stadtbibliothek Köln vorhandenen Musikdrucke des 16., 17. und 18. Jahrhunderts. 1958.

28. Hiller, F. Aus Ferdinand Hillers Briefwechsel (1826-1861); Beiträge zu einer Biographie, hrsg. von Reinhold Sietz. Teil 1. 1958. See also Heft 48 below.

29. Schwermer, J. Ewald Strässer; Leben und Werke. 1958.

30. Kremp, W. Quellen und Studien zum Responsorium prolixum in der Ueberlieferung der Euskirchener Offiziumsantiphonare. 1958.

31. Thoene, W. Friedrich Beurhaus und seine Musiktraktate, Teil I und II. 1959.

32. Wiens, H. Musik und Musikpflege am herzoglichen Hof zu Kleve. 1959.

33. Overath, J. Untersuchungen über die Melodien des Liedpsalters von Kaspar Ulenberg (Köln 1582); ein Beitrag zur Geschichte des Kirchenliedes im 16. Jahrhundert. 1960.

34. Zöllner, G. Franz Hünten; sein Leben und sein Werk. 1959.

35. Fellerer, K.G., ed. Beiträge zur Musikgeschichte

der Stadt Köln; zum 70. Geburtstag von Paul Mies. Unter
Mitarbeit von H. Hüschen, W. Kahl, K. W. Niemöller.
1959.
36. ----. Musik im niederländisch-niederdeutschen Raum.
Unter Mitarbeit von H. Blommen, K. Dreimüller, H.
Klotz, E. Klusen, M. A. Vente & H. Wiens. 1960.
37. Beiträge zur Musikgeschichte der Stadt Duisburg;
Tagungsbericht. Duisburg, 1960.
38. Beurhaus, F. Musicae rudimenta (Dortmund, 1581).
Eingeleitet und hrsg. von Walter Thoene. 1960.
39. Niemöller, K. W. Kirchenmusik und reichsstädtische
Musikpflege im Köln des 18. Jahrhunderts. 1960.
40. Steffen, G. Johann Hugo von Wilderer; Kapellmeister
am kurpfälzischen Hofe zu Düsseldorf und Mannheim.
1960.
41. Kaspersmeier, G. Wilhelm Dyckerhoff (1810-1881)
und seine Kompositionslehre. 1960.
42. Blommen, H. Anfänge und Entwicklung des Männerchorwesens am Niederrhein. 1960.
43. Fellerer, K. G., ed. Rheinische Musiker. 1. Folge.
1960. See Heft 53 below.
44. ----. Musik im Raume Remscheid. Unter Mitarbeit
von Ursula Bächer et al. 1960.
45. Pohl, R. Die Messen des Johannes Mangon. 1961.
46. Kirchrath R. Theatrum musicae choralis; das
ist Kurze und gründlich erklärte Verfassung der Are-
tinischer und Gregorianischer Singkunst. Köln am Rheine,
1782. Eingeleitet und im Faks. hrsg. von Karl Gustav
Fellerer. 1961.
47. Beurhaus, F. Erotematum musicae libri duo
(Nürnberg, 1580). Faksimiledruck mit Nachwort und
kritischem Bericht hrsg. von Walter Thoene. 1961.
48. Hiller, F. Aus Ferdinand Hillers Briefwechsel
(1862-1869); Beiträge zu einer Biographie Ferdinand
Hillers, hrsg. von Reinhold Sietz. Teil II. 1961.
See Heft 28 above.

49. Voss, B. August von Othegraven; Leben und Werke. 1961.

50. Schanppecher, M. Die Musica figurativa des Melchior Schanppecher; Opus aureum, Köln, 1501, pars III/IV. Eingeleitet und hrsg. von Klaus Wolfgang Niemöller. 1961. See Heft 11 above.

51. Strauss, R. , & F. Wüllner. Richard Strauss und Franz Wüllner im Briefwechsel. Hrsg. von D. Kämper. 1963.

52. Drux, H. , K. W. Niemöller, & W. Thoene, ed. Studien zur Musikgeschichte des Rheinlandes. 2. Folge. Karl Gustav Fellerer zum 60. Geburtstag überreicht von den Mitgliedern der Arbeitsgemeinschaft für rheinische Musikgeschichte. 1962.

53. Fellerer, K. G. , et al, ed. Rheinische Musiker. In Verband mit zahlreichen Mitarbeitern. Folge 2. 1962. See Heft 43 above.

54. Rutgerus Sycamber de Venray. Dialogus de musica (De recta, congrua devotaque cantione dialogus). Hrsg. von F. Soddemann. 1963.

55. Kämper, D. Franz Wüllner; Leben, Wirken und kompositorisches Schaffen. 1963.

56. Hiller, F. Aus Ferdinand Hillers Briefwechsel; Beiträge zu einer Biographie Ferdinand Hillers. Von Reinhold Sietz. Band 3: 1870-1875. 1964.

Beiträge zur Schulmusik. Hrsg. von Wilhelm Drangmeister und Hans Fischer.
Wolfenbüttel: Möseler

1. Martens, H. Musikdiktat und musikalisches Schreibwerk in der Schule; mit anschliessendem methodisch-didaktischem Lehrgang. 2. verb. Auflage 1957.

2. Bimberg, S. Einführung in die Musikpsychologie. 1957.

3. Münnich, R. Jale; ein Beitrag zur Tonsilbenfrage und zur Schulmusikpropädeutik. 2. Auflage. 1959.

4. Werdin, E. Rhythmisch musikalische Uebung und Anwendung des rhythmischen Instrumentariums. 1959.

5. Pape, H. Der ganzheitliche Weg im musikalischen Anfangsunterricht. 1959.
6. Schulz-Koehn, D.   Jazz in der Schule. 1959.
7. Fischer, H. Vergleichende Musikkunde. 1960.
8. Voss, O. Methodik des Musikunterrichts für das 5.-7. Schuljahr des Gymnasiums. 1961.
9. Kramarz, J. Das Streichquartett. 1961.
10. Moser, H. J.   Die Gottesdienstmusik der Protestanten. 1961.
11. Borris, S. Die Oper im 20. Jahrhundert. 1962.
12. Rauhe, H. Musikerziehung durch Jazz. 1962.
13. Berger, G. Béla Bartók. 1963.

Berliner Studien zur Musikwissenschaft. Veröffentlichungen des Musikwissenschaftlichen Instituts der Freien Universität Berlin. Hrsg. von Adam Adrio.
Berlin: Merseburger
1. Forchert, A. Das Spätwerk des Michael Praetorius; italienische und deutsche Stilbegegnung. 1959.
2. Gessner, E. Samuel Scheidts geistliche Konzerte; ein Beitrag zur Geschichte der Gattung. 1961.
3. Abraham, L. U. Der Generalbass im Schaffen des Michael Praetorius und seine harmonischen Voraussetzungen. 1961.
4. Siebenkäs, D. Ludwig Berger (1777-1839); sein Leben und Werke unter besonderer Berücksichtigung seines Liedschaffens. 1963.
5. Reckziegel, W.   Das Cantional von Johan Herman Schein; seine geschichtlichen Grundlagen. 1963.

Berner Veröffentlichungen zur Musikforschung. Begründet von Ernst Kurth.
Bern/Stuttgart: Paul Haupt
1. Zulauf, M. Die Harmonik Johann Sebastian Bachs.
2. Balmer, L. Tonsystem und Kirchentöne bei Johannes Tinctoris. 1935.
3. Zulauf, M. Der Musikunterricht in der Geschichte des bernischen Schulwesens von 1528 bis 1798. 1934.

4. Dickenmann, P. Die Entwicklung der Harmonik bei A. Skrjabin. 1935.

5. Bieri, G. Die Lieder von Hugo Wolf. 1935.

6. Tobel, R. von. Die Formenwelt der klassischen Instrumentalmusik. 1935.

7. Quervain, F. de. Der Chorstil Henri Purcells. 1935.

8. Thiele, E. Die Chorfugen Johann Sebastian Bachs. 1936.

9. Obreschkoff, C. Das bulgarische Volkslied. 1937.

10. Schnapper, E. Die Gesänge des jungen Schubert. 1937.

11. Balmer, L. Orlando di Lassos Motetten. 1938.

12. Fischer, K. von. Griegs Harmonik und die nordländische Folklore. 1938.

13. May, H. von. Die Kompositionstechnik T. L. de Victorias. 1943.

14. Vischer, D. C. Der musikgeschichtliche Traktat des Pierre Bourdelot (1610 bis 1685). 1947.

15. Kull, H. Dvořáks Kammermusik. 1948.

16. Favre-Lingorow, S. Der Instrumentalstil von Purcell. 1950.

17. Biber, W. Das Problem der Melodieformel in der einstimmigen Musik des Mittelalters dargestellt und entwickelt am Lutherchoral. 1951.

Further volumes appear within the series: Publikationen der Schweizerischen Musikforschenden Gesellschaft.

Beroemde musici

's-Gravenhage: J. Philip Kruseman

1. Couturier, L. Beethoven. 1926. 3e druk.

2. Keller, G. Bach. 2e druk. 1936.

3. Hutschenruyter, W. Chopin. 1926. 3e druk 1949.

4. Santen, R. van. Debussy. 2e druk, herzien, bijgewerkt en aangevuld door B. v. d. Sigtenhorst Meyer. 1947.

5. Keller, G. Schubert. 1927. 3e druk 1951.

6. Hutschenruyter, W. Mahler. 1927.

7. Hutschenruyter, W. Mozart. 1927. 2e druk 1942.
8. Wessem, C. van. Liszt. 1927. 2e druk.
9. Abert, H. Schumann. 1928.
10. Hutschenruyter, W. Wagner. 1928.
11. Wessem, C. van. Moderne franse musici. 1928.
12. Hutschenruyter, W. Brahms. 1929.
13. Dalen, H. van. Russische muziek en componisten. 1930. 2e druk.
14. Kapp, J. Paganini.
15. Hutschenruyter, W. Richard Strauss. 1929.
16. Sanders, P. F. Moderne nederlandse componisten. 1931?
17. Dalen, H. van. Tsjaikofsky. 1930. 2e druk.
18. Keller, G. Händel.
19. Röntgen, J. Grieg.
20. Mueren, F. van der. Vlaamsche muziek en componisten in de XIXde en XXste eeuw. 1931.
21. Keller, G. Haydn. 1932.
22. Backers, C. Nederlandse componisten van 1400 tot onze tijd. 1941. 2e druk 1948.
23. Onnen, F. Debussy als criticus en essayist. 1948.
24. Prick van Wely, M. Chopin als mens en musicus.

Bibliografia polskich czasopism muzycznych.
Kraków: PWM
1. Strumiłło, D. Tygodnik muzyczny 1820-21; Pamiętnik muzyczny warszawski 1835-36. 1955.
2. Michałowski, K. Gazeta teatralna 1843-44. 1956.
3. Bogdany, W., & K. Michałowski. Ruch muzyczny 1857-62. 1957.
4. Bogdany, W. Gazeta muzyczna i teatralna 1865-66; Przegląd muzyczny 1877. 1955.
5. Poźniak, W. Echo muzyczne, teatralne i artystyczne 1879-1907. T. 1. In prep.
6. Michałowska, M. Nowości muzyczne 1903-14; Lutnista 1905-07. 1962.

7. Porębowiczowa, A. Młoda muzyka 1908-09; Przegląd muzyczny 1910-14, 1918-19. 1964?

8. Kielanowska-Bronowicz, M. Kwartalnik muzyczny 1911-14, 1928-33, 1948-50; Polski rocznik muzykologiczny 1935-36. 1963.

9. Michałowski, K. Muzyka 1925-38. T.1, 1962. T.2, 1963.

10. Świderska, J. Lwowskie wiadomości muzyczne i literackie 1925-34; Szopen 1932; Echo 1936-37. 1962.

11. Porębowiczowa, A. Przegląd muzyczny poznański 1925-31; Życie muzyczne i teatralne 1934-35. 1964?

12. Bogdany, W. Muzyka polska 1934-39. In prep.

13. Prokopowicz, M. Gazetka muzyczna 1936-39; Muzyka współczesna 1936-39; Chopin 1937. 1961.

Biblioteca di cultura ceciliana
Roma: Associazione Italiana Santa Cecilia per la Musica Sacra

1. Eccher, C. Problemi didattico-organizzativi delle scuole ceciliane. 1957.

2. Statuto e Regolamento dell'A. I. S. C. 1957.

3. Alcini, I. Pio XII e la musica. 1957.

4. Lorenzo Perosi; sacerdote e artista. 1958.

5. Pio XII. Lettera enciclica "Musicae sacrae disciplina" (testo latino-italiano). 1958?

6. Gajard, J. Les débuts de la restauration grégorienne à Solesmes. 1958.

7. ----. Quelques réflexions sur les premières formes de la musique sacrée. 1958.

8. Matteucci, B. Teologia della musica sacra. 1958.

9. ----. La musica sacra come espressione concreta e completa della caritas cristiana. 1958.

10. Taddei, N. Problemi della musica come arte sacra. 1958.

11. Istruzione sulla musica sacra e la sacra liturgia, secondo il pensiero delle encicliche di Pio XII "Musicae

sacrae disciplina" e "Mediator dei" (testo originale latino e versione italiana). 1958.

Nos. 3 & 5-10 are included in L'enciclica "Musicae sacrae disciplina" di Sua Santità Pio XII; testo e commento, a cura dell'Associazione italiana S. Cecilia. Roma: A.I.S. C., 1957.

Biblioteca di cultura musicale. A cura di Giovanni Cavicchioli. Modena, Parma: Ugo Guanda

1 & 2. See series: I Grandi musicisti.

3. Machabey, A. Maurice Ravel. Versione a cura di Wanda Lopez. 1951.

4. Vallas, L. Achille-Claude Debussy. Versione a cura di Wanda Lopez. 1952.

5. Valabrega, C. Il clavicembalista Domenico Scarlatti; il suo secolo, la sua opera. 1937. 2. ed. 1955.

6. Rognoni, L. Rossini. 1956.

7. Pastura, F. Bellini secondo la storia. 1959.

8. Pasi, M. George Gershwin. In collaborazione con Gerardo Rusconi. 1958.

Biblioteca sansoniana musicale
Firenze, Bologna: Sansoni

1. Roncaglia, G. L'ascensione creatrice di Giuseppe Verdi. 1940. 2. ed. 1951.

2. Paoli, R. Debussy. 1940. 2. ed. 1952.

3. Rensis, R. de. Arrigo Boito; capitoli biografici. 1942.

4. Fragapane, P. Spontini. 2. ed.? 1954.

Seconda serie. Only Ottavio Tiby, La musica in Grecia e a Roma (Firenze: Sansoni, 1942) identified. Probably no others appeared.

Biblioteka Chopinowska. Pod redakcją Mieczysława Tomaszewskiego. Kraków: PWM

1. Kleczyński, J. O wykonywaniu dzieł Chopina. 1960.

2. Chopin, F. Kompozytorzy polscy o Fryderyku Chopinie; antologia. [Ed. and Preface by] Mieczysław Tomaszewski. 1959.

3. Liszt, F. Fryderyk Chopin. Tłum. [z franc.] Maria Traczewska. 1960.

4. Bronarski, L. Szkice chopinowskie. Tłum. [z franc.] Maria Traczewska. 1961.

5. Hoesick, F. Chopin; życie i twórczość. T. 1: Warszawa 1810-1831. 1962. T. 2: Pierwsze lata w Paryżu, 1831-1838; George Sand, 1838-1848. 1964. T. 3: Rozdźwięki, 1845-1848; Nella miseria, 1848-49. T. 4: Kopernik fortepianu. In prep.

6. Kobylańska, Krystyna. Rękopisy muzyczne Chopina; katalog autografów i kopii. In prep.

7. Wiersze o Chopinie; antologia i bibliografia. [Ed. by] Edmund Słuszkiewicz. [Preface by] Julian Przyboś. In prep.

8. Mazel, L. Studia chopinowskie. Tłum. Jerzy Popiel. In prep.

9. Niecks, F. Chopin; człowiek i muzyk. Tłum. Małgorzata Szerchowa. In prep.

10. Idzikowski, M., & B. E. Sydow. Portret Chopina; antologia ikonograficzna. Wyd. 2. 1963.

Biblioteka "Muzikalno teatralno, i izobrazitelno izkustva"
Sofia: Tsentr. K-T na DKMS, Otd. "Propaganda i agitat-siîa"

1. Siârov, P. Kratŭk muzikalen rechnik. 1961.

2. Stŭrshenov, B. Bŭlgarska simfonichna muzika. 1961.

3. Kolev, B. Veliki ispanski khudozhnitski; Greko, Ribera, Velaskes i Goîîa. 1961. Non-music.

4. Kaufman, N. Bŭlgarska narodna musika. 1961.

Biblioteka słuchacza koncertowego. Redaktor cyklu: Mieczysław Tomaszewski.
Kraków: PWM
Seria wprowadzająca

1. Habela, J. Słowniczek muzyczny. 1956. Wyd. 2. 1958. Wyd. 3. 1962.
2. Chodkowski, A. Instrumenty orkiestry dzisiejszej. 1956. Wyd. 2. 1960.
3. Hanuszewska, M. 1000 Kompozytorów. 1961. Wyd. 2. 1963.

Seria biograficzna
1. Strumiłło, T. Juliusz Zarębski. 1954.
2. Sutkowski, A. Zgymunt Noskowski. 1957.
3. Kański, J. Ludomir Różycki. 1955.
4. Golachowski, S. Karol Szymanowski. 1956.
5. Jachimecki, Z. Władysław Żeleński. 1959.
6. Opieński, H. Ignacy Jan Paderewski. 1960.
7. Stromenger, K. Fryderyk Chopin. 1959.
8. Iwaszkiewicz, J. Jan Sebastian Bach. 1963.

Seria wokalna
1. Szweykowski, Z. M. Kultura wokalna XVI-wiecznej Polski. 1957.
2. Jachimecki, Z. , & W. Poźniak. Antoni Radziwiłł i jego muzyka do "Fausta." 1957.

Seria symfoniczna
4. Haraschin, S. Koncerty fortepianowe Beethovena. 1954.
7. Strumiłło, T. Uwertury Kurpińskiego. 1954.
11. ----. Koncerty skrzypcowe Wieniawskiego. 1955.
12. Zieliński, T. Ostatnie symfonie Czajkowskiego. 1955.
13. Młodziejowski, J. Moja ojczyzna Smetany. 1957.
14. Bronowicz, T. Concerty Brahmsa. 1955.
16. Kisielewski, S. Poematy symfoniczne Straussa. 1955?
17. Marek, T. Poematy symfoniczne Mieczysława Karłowicza. 1959.
18. Zieliński, T. Koncerty Prokofiewa. 1959.
   Frączkiewicz, A.   Koncerty Chopina.

Bibliotheca musica
Budapest: Zeneműkiadó Vállalat

1-2. Szelényi, I. A magyar zene története. 2 vols. 1959.
3. Várnai, P. A lengyel zene története. 1959.
4. Sárai, T. A cseh zene története. 1959.
5. Vámosi Nagy, I., & P. Várnai. Bánk Bán az opera-szinpadon; operadramaturgiai tanulmány. 1960.
6-7. Pándi, M. Az olasz zene története. 2 vols. 1960.
8. Sochacki, S. A. Liszt Ferenc és a lengyelek. 1963.
9. Heszke, B. A román zene története. 1963.
10. Nejedlý, Z. Válogatott zenei tanulmányok. 1963

Bibliotheca musicae. Collana di cataloghi e bibliografie
diretta da Claudio Sartori.
Milano: Istituto Editoriale Italiano
1. Assisi. La cappella della Basilica di S. Francesco. 1.
Catalogo del fondo musicale nella Biblioteca Comunale
di Assisi, a cura di Claudio Sartori. Prefazione di P.
Giuseppe Zaccaria. 1962.

Black Bull Chapbooks
Victoria (Vol. 1), Ferntree Gully, (Vol. 2/), Australia:
Rams Skull Press
1. Anderson, H., ed. The Dying Stockman; A Ballad.
1954.
2. ----. Two Songs of '57. 1954.
3. ----. Botany Bay Broadsides. 1956.
4. ----. Songs of Billy Barlow. 1956.
5. Ward, R. B. Three Street Ballads. 1957.
6. Manifold, J. S. The Violin, Banjo & the Bones; An
Essay on the Instruments of Bush Music. 1957.
7. Anderson, H., ed. Australian Song Index, 1828-1956.
1957.

Bŭlgarska Akademiiă na Naukite. Trudove na Instituta za Muzik:
Sofia: Bŭlgarska Akademiiă na Naukite
1. Motsev, A. D. Ritŭm i takt v bŭlgarskata narodna
muzika. 1949.

Les Cahiers du Journal Musical Français
Paris: Société française de Diffusion Musicale et Artistique
1. Hofmann, R. La danse. Avant-propos de Serge Lifar. 1952.
2. Petit, P.   Autour de la chanson populaire. 1952.
3. Pincherle, M. Le petit lexique des termes musicaux d'usage courant. 1953.
4. Vuillermoz, E. Les instruments de l'orchestre. 1953.
5. Hofmann, R. Serge Lifar et son ballet. Avant-propos de Thamar Karsavina. 1953?
6. ----. Petite histoire de la musique russe. 1953.
7. Manuel, R., pseud. Comment écoutez-vous la musique? 1953.
8. Gavoty, B.   Deux capitales romantiques: Vienne, Paris. 1953.
9. Feschotte, J. Musique et poésie; libres-propos. 1953.
10. Hofmann, R. Naissance d'un ballet. 1954.
11. Not published.
12. Goléa, A. L'avènement de la musique classique de Bach à Mozart. 1955.
13. Alain, O. La musique de chambre. 1955.
15. Lonchampt, J. Les quatuors à cordes de Beethoven. 1956.
Hofmann, R. La musique en Russie des origines à nos jours. 1956. Unnumbered.

Catalogue des oeuvres de compositeurs belges. Fonds Daniele Cohen-Deswarte.
Bruxelles: Centre Belge de Documentation Musicale
1. Francis de Bourguignon. 1953.
2. Gérard Bertouille. 1953.
3. Victor Legley. 1953.
4. Marcel Poot. 1953.
5. Joseph Jongen. 1953.
6. Lodewijk Mortelmans. 1954.

7. Albert Huybrechts. 1954.

8. Raymond Moulaert. 1954.

9. Arthur Meulemans. 1954.

10. Willem Pelemans. 1954.

11. Flor Alpaerts. 1954.

12. Maurice Schoemaker. 1954.

13. François Rasse. 1954.

14. Raymond Chevreuille. 1955.

15. Armand Marsick. 1955.

16. Gaston Brenta. 1955.

17. Michel Brusselmans. 1956.

18. August Baeyens. 1956.

19. Robert Herberigs. 1957.

20. Jean Absil. 1957.

Catalogue of Works by Members of the Composers' Guild
   of Great Britain
Cheltenham: Composer's Guild of Great Britain
1. British Orchestral Music. 1958.

Catalogus musicus. Hrsg. von der Internationalen Vereini-
   gung der Musikbibliotheken und der Internationalen
   Gesellschaft für Musikwissenschaft.
Kassel: Internationale Vereinigung der Musikbibliotheken
Riedel, F. W. Das Musikarchiv im Minoritenkonvent zu
   Wien (Katalog des älteren Bestandes vor 1784). 1963.
Becherini, B. I Manoscritti rinascimentali della Biblioteca
   della Conservatorio "L. Cherubini" di Firenze.
Schaal, R. Das Inventar der Kantorei St. Anna in Augsburg.
Layer, A. Katalog des Augsburger Verlegers Lotter von
   1753.
Kümmerling, H. Katalog der Musiksammlung Bokemeyer.
Schaal, R. Kaspar Flurschütz; Musikalienkataloge, Augs-
   burg 1613-1624.
Bacq, J. , & J. Robijns. Le "Fonds Ste. Gudule" au Con-
   servatoire Royal de Bruxelles.

Lesure, F. Bibliographie des éditions d'Estienne Roger
et Michel Charles Le Cène.
All in progress

Catholic University of America Studies in Music
Washington, D. C.: Catholic University of America Press
1. Stauffer, D. W. Intonation Deficiencies of Wind Instruments in Ensemble. 1954.
2. Canave, P. C. G. A Re-evaluation of the Role Played
by Carl Philipp Emmanuel Bach in the Development of
the Clavier Sonata. 1956.
3. Durham, G. D. The Development of the German Concert
Overture. 1957.
4. Connor, Sister M. J. B. Gregorian Chant and Medieval
Hymn Tunes in the Works of J. S. Bach. 1957.
5. Klein, Sister M. J. The Contribution of Daniel Gregory
Mason to American Music. 1957.
6. Wells, L. J. A History of the Music Festival at Chau-
tauqua Institution from 1874 to 1957. 1958.
7. Lefkoff, G. Five Sixteenth Century Venetian Lute Books.
1960.
8. Foelber, P. F. Bach's Treatment of the Subject of
Death in His Choral Music. 1961.
9. Keane, Sister M. M. The Theoretical Writings of Jean-
Philippe Rameau. 1961.

The Choirmaster's Notebook Series
Philadelphia: Fortress Press
C 1. Nordin, H. W. Choral Conducting; Learning and
Teaching. Ed. by Dayton W. Nordin. 1963.
C 2. Groom, L. R., & D. W. Nordin. Choral Conducting;
Learning and Teaching. Ed. by Dayton W. Nordin. 1963.
Church Music Society. Occasional Papers.
London: Oxford University Press
Vols. 1-15 (1913-42)
16. Arnold, J. H. The Music of the Holy Com-

munion. 1946.

17. Armstrong, T. Church Music Today. 1946.
18. Conway, M. P. Organ Voluntaries. 1948.
19. Statham, H. Restoration Church Music. 1949.
20. Lovett, S. H. The Use of Small Church Organs. 1952.
21. Shaw, H. W. Eighteenth-Century Cathedral Music. 1952.
22. ----. From Tallis to Tomkins; a Survey of Church Music, c. 1550- c. 1650. With a Foreword by the Very Rev. A. S. Duncan-Jones. 1954.
23. Hymns and Their Tunes. Reprinted from the Report of Archbishops' Committee, 1957.

Church Music Society. Shorter Papers.
London: H. Milford, later Oxford University Press
1. Church Music Society, London. Music in Village Churches. 1917?
2. Gardener, G. Music in Larger Country and Smaller Town Churches. 1917.
3. Grace, H. Music in Parish Churches. 1917.
4. Roberts, R. E. Hints on Hymn Tunes.
5. Daly, C. E. Congregational Hymn Practices.
6. Kelk, A. H. Singing of the Psalms and Canticles to Anglican Chants.
7. Stewart, E. Points of View. 1932.
8. Arnold, J. H. The Music of the Holy Communion. 1933. Rewritten as Occasional Papers, No. 16 (1946).
9. Conway, M. P. Organ Playing.
10. Anonymous member of the Society of the Sacred Mission. Music of the Parish Church.

The Church Musician's Bookshelf
Toledo, Ohio: Gregorian Institute of America
Series 1
1. Shebbeare, A. Choral Recitation of the Divine Office; A Guide to Choir Directors. 1955.

2. Carroll, J.R. A Choirmaster's Guide to Holy Week.
1957.

Series 2

1. Carroll, J.R. The Technique of Gregorian Chironomy.
1955.

2. Institut Gregorien, Paris. An Applied Course in Gregorian Chant. Translated and edited from the official course
syllabus of the Gregorian Institute of Paris by Joseph
Robert Carroll. 1956.

3. Mary Demetria, Sister. Basic Gregorian Chant and Sight
Reading. 1957.

4. ----. Basic Gregorian Chant and Sight Reading;
Movable do Edition. 1960.

Colección Labor; Biblioteca de iniciación cultural. Sección
V: Música.

Barcelona: Editorial Labor. Mostly translations.

15. Scholz, H. Compendio de armonía. 3a ed. 1933. 4a
ed. 1951.

68. Riemann, H. Compendio de instrumentación. 2a ed.
1930.

112. Sachs, C. La música en la antigüedad. 1927. 2a ed.
1934.

126. López Chavarri, E. Música popular española. 1927.
2a ed. 1940. 3a ed. 1958.

143. Riemann, H. Bajo cifrado (Armonía al piano). 2a ed.
1951.

150. ----. Reducción al piano de la partitura de orquesta.
2a ed. 1932.

155/56. Volbach, F. La orquesta moderna. 2a ed.

162. Riemann, H. Fraseo musical. 2a ed.

172. ----. Teoría general de la música. 2a ed. 1932.
3a ed.

173. ----. Dictado musical. 2a ed. 1953.

182. ----. Manual del pianista. 2a ed. 1951.

205. ----. Manual del organista. 1929.

211/12. ----. Composición musical. 1929. 2a ed. 1950.

229. Krehl, S. Fuga. 2a ed. 1953.

230. ----. Contrapunto. 2a ed. 1940. 3a ed. 1953.

244/45. Riemann, H. Historia de la música. 2a ed. 1934. 3a ed. in prep.

264. Wellesz, E. Música bizantina. 1930.

265/66. Riemann, H. Armonía y modulación. 2a ed.

284. Lachmann, R. Música de Oriente. 1931.

285. Toch, E.   La melodía. 1931.

319. Subirá, J.   La tonadilla escénica. 1933.

408/09. Araiz Martínez, A. Historia de la música religiosa en España. 1942.

416/17. Zamacois, J. Tratado de armonía. I. 1945. 2a ed.

419. Prado, G. El canto gregoriano. 1945.

429. Subirá, J. Historia de la música teatral en España. 1945.

430/31. Zamacois, J. Tratado de armonía. II. 1946. 2a ed.

436/38. ----. Tratado de armonía. III. 1948. 2a ed. 1958.

450. ----. Teoría general de la música. I. 1949. 2a ed. 1952. 4a ed. 1963.

469. ----. Teoría general de la música. II.

494/96. Mantecón Molins, J. J.   Introducción al estudio de la música. 2a ed.

497. Manén, J. El violín.

Cuartero, A. Método de canto.

The volumes in Colección Labor are numbered consecutively through all thirteen series, of which Música comprises series five.

Collana di "Musica jazz"
Milano: Messaggerie Musicali
1. Barazzetta, G. Jazz inciso in Italia. 1960.

Collana di Studi palestriniani
Roma: Centro di Studi Palestriniani
1. Ferracci, E. Il Palestrina; documenti di vita, prob-

lemi e prospettive d'arte. 1960.

2-3 Paccagnella, Ė. La formazione del linguaggio musicale
Parte Ia: Il canto gregoriano. 1961. Parte IIa: J. S.
Bach. 1962.

Collection des biographies pratiques à l'usage des ėtudiants
en musique
Chambėry: Éditions Lire
1. Meyer, M. -A. J. -Ph. Rameau; J. S. Bach. 1946.
2. ----. R. Schumann. 1946.
3. ----. Van Beethoven. 1946.

Collection d'ėtudes musicologiques; Sammlung musikwissenschaftlicher Abhandlungen. Fondėe par Karl Nef.
Strasbourg: Éditions P. H. Heitz
1. Pirro, A. La musique à Paris sous le règne de Charles
VI (1380-1422). 1930. 2. ėd. 1958.
2. Sieber, P. Johann Friedrich Reichardt als Musikästhe-
tiker; seine Anschauungen über Wesen und Wirkung der
Musik. 1930.
3. Lüthy, W. Mozart und die Tonartencharakteristik. 1931.
4. Schubert, K. Spontinis italienische Schule. 1932.
5. Meyer-Baer, K. Bedeutung und Wesen der Musik. 1932.
6. Fellerer, K. G. Beiträge zur Choralbegleitung und
Choralverarbeitung in der Orgelmusik des ausgehenden
18. und beginnenden 19. Jahrhunderts. 1932.
7. Hegar, E. Die Anfänge der neueren Musikgeschichts-
schreibung um 1770 bei Gerbert, Burney und Hawkins.
1932.
8. Pinthus, G.   Das Konzertleben in Deutschland; ein
Abriss seiner Entwicklung bis zum Beginn des 15. [i. e.
19.] Jahrhunderts. 1932.
9. Saam, J. Zur Geschichte des Klavierquartetts bis in
die Romantik. 1933.
10. Müller, G. Daniel Steibelt; sein Leben und seine
Klavierwerke (Etüden und Sonaten). 1933.
11. Hamel, F. Die Psalmkompositionen Johann Rosenmüllers.

1933.

12. Krüger, L. Die hamburgische Musikorganisation im
XVII. Jahrhundert. 1933.

13. Hol, J. C. Horatio Vecchi's Weltliche Werke. 1934.

14. Jammers, E. Das Karlsoffizium "Regali natus";
Einführung, Text und Uebertragung in moderne Notenschrift. 1934.

15. Wolff, E. G. Grundlagen einer autonomen Musikästhetik.
1934. See Bd. 27 below.

16. Schneider, M. F. Beiträge zu einer Anleitung Clavichord
und Cembalo zu spielen. 1934.

17. Keh, C. S. Die koreanische Musik; Einführung und Be-
sprechung von 17 zum ersten mal in die europäische
Notenschrift übertragenen Kompositionen. 1935.

18. Balet, L. Die Verbürgerlichung der deutschen Kunst,
Literatur und Musik im 18. Jahrhundert. 1936.

19. Liess, A. Claude Debussy; das Werk im Zeitbild. 2
Bd. 1936.

20. Fallet, É. M. La vie musicale au pays de Neuchâtel du
XIIIe à la fin du XVIII siècle; contribution à l'histoire
de la musique en Suisse. Préface de Gustave Doret.
1936.

21. Bukofzer, M. F. Geschichte des englischen Diskants und
des Fauxbourdons nach den theoretischen Quellen. 1936.

22. Dannemann, E. Die spätgotische Musiktradition in
Frankreich und Burgund vor dem Auftreten Dufays.
1936.

23. Augustinus, A. Die Musik. Erste deutsche Uebertragung
von Carl Johann Perl. 1937.

24. Apel, W. Accidentien und Tonalität in den Musikdenk-
mälern des 15. und 16. Jahrhunderts. 1937.

25. Jammers, E. Der gregorianische Rhythmus; antiphonale
Studien. 1937.

26. Albersheim, G. Zur Psychologie der Ton- und Klangei-
genschaften. 1939.

27. Wolff, E. G. Grundlagen einer autonomen Musikästhetik.

T. 2. 1938. See Bd. 15 above.

28. Bartenstein, H. Hector Berlioz' Instrumentationskunst und ihre geschichtlichen Grundlagen. 1939.

28. Marix, J. Histoire de la musique et des musiciens de la cour de Bourgogne sous le règne de Philippe le Bon (1420-1467). 1939. Presumably should read Bd. 29.

30. Fischer, K. von. Die Beziehungen von Form und Motiv in Beethovens Instrumentalwerken. 1948.

31. Jammers, E. Anfänge der abendländischen Musik. 1955.

32. Schering, A. Humor, Heldentum, Tragik bei Beethoven. Vorwort von Helmuth Osthoff. 1955.

33. Galpin, F. W. The Music of the Sumerians and Their Immediate Successors, the Babylonians and Assyrians. 2nd ed. 1955.

34. Hickmann, H. Musicologie pharaonique; études sur l'évolution de l'art musical dans l'Égypte ancienne. 1956.

35. Jacobi, E. R. Die Entwicklung der Musiktheorie in England nach der Zeit von Jean-Philippe Rameau. I. 1957. See Heft 39 below.

36. Fischer, H. Schallgeräte in Ozeanien; Bau und Spieltechnik, Verbreitung und Funktion. 1958.

37. Hickmann, H. , & Charles Grégoire, Duc de Mecklembourg. Catalogue d'Enregistrements de musique folklorique égyptienne, précédé d'un rapport préliminaire sur les traces de l'art musical pharaonique dans la mélopée de la Vallée du nil. 1958.

38. Leuchtmann, H. Die musikalischen Wortausdeutungen in den Motetten des Magnum Opus Musicum von Orlando di Lasso. 1959.

39. Jacobi, E. R. Die Entwicklung der Musiktheorie in England nach der Zeit des Jean-Philippe Rameau. II. 1960. III. Faksimile-Ergänzungsband. See Heft 35 above.

40. Carl Gregor, Herzog zu Mecklenburg. Aegyptische Rhythmik; Rhythmen und Rhythmusinstrumente im heutigen Aegypten. 1960.

41. Neumann, F.-H. Die Aesthetik des Rezitativs; zur Theorie des Rezitativs im 17. und 18. Jahrhundert. 1962.
42. Kolneder, W. Die Solokonzertform bei Vivaldi. 1961.
43. Laade, W. Die Struktur der korsischen Lamento-Melodik. 1962.
44. Holler, K. H. Giovanni Maria Bononcinis "Musico prattico" in seiner Bedeutung für die musikalische Satzlehre des 17. Jahrhunderts. 1963.
45. Carl Gregor, Herzog zu Mecklenburg, & W. Scheck. Die Theorie des Blues in modernen Jazz. 1963.

Collection Euterpe. Dirigée par Norbert Dufourcq.
Paris: La Colombe, Éditions du Vieux Colombier. Partly numbered.
 1. Favre, G. Paul Dukas; sa vie, son oeuvre. 1948.
 2. Ferchault, G. Claude Debussy; musicien français. 1948.
 3. Bernard, R. Albert Roussel; sa vie, son oeuvre. 1948.
 4. Gardien, J. Jean-Philippe Rameau. 1949.
 5. Dufourcq, N. César Franck; le milieu, l'oeuvre, l'art. 1949.
 6. Rostand, C. Richard Strauss; l'ambiance, les origines, la vie, l'oeuvre, l'esthétique et le style. 1949.
 7. Borrel, E. Jean-Baptiste Lully; le cadre, la vie, l'oeuvre. 1949.
 8. Prod'homme, J. G. François-Joseph Gossec (1734-1829); la vie, les oeuvres, l'homme, et l'artiste. 1949.
 9. Coeuroy, A. Robert Schumann. 1950.

Collection "Les documents célèbres"
Lausanne: Éditions du Cervin
 1. Strauss, R. Anecdotes et souvenirs. Version française de Pierre Meylan et Jean Schneider; textes réunis par Willi Schuh. 1951.

2. Beethoven, L. van. Les plus belles lettres de Beethoven; l'ami, l'amant, l'artiste. Choix et traduction de Jean Schneider. 1951.
3. Perlemuter, V. , & H. Jourdan-Morhange. Ravel d'après Ravel. 1953.
4. Mozart, W. A. Les plus belles lettres de Mozart. Choix et traduction nouvelle de Pierre Meylan.
5. Indy, V. d', H. Duparc, & A. Roussel. Lettres à Auguste Sérieyx. Recueillies et publiées par M. L. Sérieyx. 1961.

Collection Triptyque. Subseries: Musique.
Paris: Richard Masse
1. Machabey, A. Maurice Ravel. 1947.
2. Saeler's [sic] Wells Company. La création de l'opéra anglais et "Peter Grimes." Publiés sous la direction de Eric Crozier; traduits de l'anglais "Opera in English" par C. Ormore. "Peter Grimes," par Annie Brierre. 1947.
3. Chantavoine, J. Camille Saint-Saëns. 1947.
4. Moreux, S. Béla Bartók; sa vie, ses oeuvres, son langage. Préface d'Arthur Honegger. 1949.

Collezione "Euterpe"
Roma: Editrice Faro
1. Valabrega, C. Il piccolo dizionario musicale per tutti. 1949.
2. Chantavoine, J. Guida dell'amatore di musica sinfonica. 1949.

Collezione "Letteratura musicale"
Milano: Fratelli Bocca Editori, later Editore Feltrinelli (Vol. 20-)
Volumes 1-18 to 1941.
19. Damilano, P.   G. Giovenale Ancina e la lauda cinquecentesca. 1953.

Further volumes in preparation in la casa editrice Feltrinelli.

Les Colloques de Wégimont. Includes subseries: Ethnomusicologie.

Château de Wégimont (Liège), Belgium: Various publishers
1. Les Colloques de Wégimont, cercle international d'études ethno-musicologiques. Premier colloque [Septembre 1954]. Rédacteur en chef, Paul Collaer. Bruxelles: Elsevier, 1956.
2. Les Colloques de Wégimont. II, 1955. L'Ars nova; recueil d'études sur la musique du XIVe siècle. (Bibliothèque de la Faculté de philosophie et lettres de l'Université de Liège, fasc. 1949.) Paris: Les Belles Lettres, 1959.
3. ----. Ethnomusicologie 2, 1956. Rédacteur en chef, Paul Collaer. Paris: Les Belles Lettres, 1960.
4. ----. Ethnomusicologie 3. Rédacteur en chef, Paul Collaer. In prep.

Columbia University Studies in Musicology
New York: Columbia University Press
1. Nef, K. An Outline of the History of Music. Trans. by Carl F. Pfatteicher. 1935.
2. Brennecke, E., Jr. John Milton the Elder and His Music. 1938.
3. Pratt, W. S. The Music of the French Psalter of 1562. 1939.
4. Upton, W. T. Anthony Philip Heinrich; A Nineteenth-Century Composer in America. 1939.
5. Johnson, H. E. Musical Interludes in Boston, 1795-1830. 1943.
6. Lowinsky, E. E. Secret Chromatic Art in the Netherlands Motet. Trans. from the German by Carl Buchman. 1946.
7. Bartók, B., & A. B. Lord. Serbo-Croatian Folk Songs;

Texts and Transcriptions of Seventy-Five Folk Songs
from the Milman Parry Collection and a Morphology of
Serbo-Croatian Folk Melodies. With a Foreword by George
Herzog. 1951.
No further volumes currently in progress.

The Commonwealth and International Library of Science,
   Technology, Engineering and Liberal Studies. Music Div.
Oxford: Pergamon Press; N.Y.: Macmillan
1. Wright, D. The Complete Bandmaster. 1963.
2-3. Illing, R. Pergamon Dictionary of Musicians and
   Music. Part 1: Musicians. Part 2: Music. 2 vols.
4. Stoll, D.G. Music Festivals of the World; A Guide
   to Leading Festivals of Music, Opera and Ballet.
   1963.
5. Baker, G. The Common Sense of Singing. 1963.

Componisten-Serie
Haarlem: Gottmer
1. Berkel, C. van. Carl Maria von Weber. 1948.
2. Thysse, W.H. Jozef Haydn. 1948.
3. Loeser, N. Richard Wagner. 1948.
4. Berkel, C. van. Paganini. 1948.
5. Loeser, N. Verdi. 1948.
6. Muller, H.J.M. Johannes Brahms. 1948.
7. Cuypers, J. Grieg. 1948.
8. Hengel, W. van. Anton Bruckner. 1948.
9. Muller, H.J.M. Tsjaikofsky. 1949.
10. Schouwman, H. Sibelius. 1949.
11. Loeser, N. Beethoven. 1950.
12. Stam, H. Robert Schumann. 1950.
13. Brandts Buys, H. Johann Sebastian Bach. 1950.
14. Berkel, C. van. Rossini. 1950.
15. Loeser, N. Gustav Mahler. 1950.
16. Pols, A.M. Franz Liszt. 1950.
17. Monnikendam, M. Igor Strawinsky. 1951.

18. Kat, A. I. M. Palestrina. 1951.
19. Geraedts, H. Béla Bartók. 1952.
20. Kuringer, P. Johann Strauss. 1952.
21. Verbeke, R. Berlioz. 1952.
22. Loeser, N. Moussorgsky. 1952.
23. Wagemans, H. Franz Schubert. 1952.
24. Koole, A. Felix Mendelssohn-Bartholdy. 1953.
25. Loeser, N. Mozart. 1953.
26. ----. Chopin. 1954.
27. Douliez, P. Claude Debussy. 1954.
28. Ravenzwaaij, G. van. Purcell. 1954.
29. Douliez, P. Peter Benoit. 1955.
30. Rutters, H. Handel. 1955.
31. Loeser, N. Wolf. 1955.
32. Prick van Wely, M. A. Dvořák. 1956.
33. Doorninck, M. van. Puccini. 1956.
34. Geraedts, J. Ravel. 1957.
35. Corredor, J. M. Casals. 1958.
36. Ewen, D. Gershwin. 1958.

Los Compositores de música
Habana: Sociedad Colombista Panamericana
 1. Marco, H. , & G. Blanch. La Bohème. Prólogo de
 Rafael Marquina. 1958.

Conseil International de la Musique; International Music
 Council; Internationaler Musikrat. Répertoires internationaux de musique contemporaine à l'usage des amateurs
 et des jeunes. Publiés par l'Association Internationale
 des Bibliothéques Musicales.
Frankfurt, London, N. Y.: Peters
 1. Musique symphonique; Symphonic Music; Symphonische
 Musik, 1880-1954. Avant-propos de Benjamin Britten,
 Préface de Samuel Baud-Bovy, publié, avec une introduction et des tables par Vladimir Fédorov. 1957.

Consejo Superior de Investigaciones Científicas, Instituto
Español de Musicología. Monografías.
Barcelona: C. S. I. C.
1. Schneider, M. El origen musical de los animales
   símbolos en la mitología y la escultura antiguas. 1946.
2. Espinós Moltó, V. El Quijote en la música. Con prólogo de José María Pemán. 1947.
3. Schneider, M. La danza de espadas y la tarantela.
   Contribución musical, etnográfico-arqueólogica al problema de los ritos en medicina. 1948.
4. ----. El Teatro del Real Palacio (1849-1851). Madrid,
   1950.
5. Subirá, J.   El compositor Iriarte (1750-1791) y el
   cultivo español del Melólogo (Melodrama). 2 vols. 1949
   & 1950.
6. Miscelánea en homenaje a Mons. Higinio Anglés. 2
   vols. 1958 & 1961.

Corpus scriptorum de musica
Roma: American Institute of Musicology
1. Johannis Affligemensis. De Musica cum Tonario, edidit
   J. Smits van Waesberghe. 1950.
2. Aribo. De Musica, edidit Joseph Smits van Waesberghe.
   1951.
3. Jacobus Leodiensis. Speculum Musicae, edidit Roger
   Bragard. Vol. 1: 1955, Vol. 2: 1961; Vol. 3: 1964; Vols.
   4-7 in prep.
4. Guido Aretinus. Micrologus, edidit Joseph Smits van
   Waesberghe. 1955.
5. Anonymus. Notitia del valore delle note del canto
   misurato, edidit Armen Carapetyan. 1957.
6. Marchettus de Padua. Pomerium, edidit Giuseppe Vecchi. 1961.
7. Ugolinus Urbevetanis. Declaratio Musicae disciplinae,
   edidit Albertus Seay. Vol. 1: 1959; Vol. 2: 1960; Vol.
   3: 1963.

8. Philippe de Vitry. Ars Nova, edidit André Gilles, Jean Maillard, & Gilbert Reaney. 1964.

9. Anon. Treatise from the Codex Vatican, Lat. 5129 (ca. 1400), edidit Albertus Seay. 1964.

10. Johannis Octobi (John Hothby). Tres Tractatuli contra Bartholomeus Ramum, edidit Albertus Seay. 1964.

Čtení o hudbě

Praha: Panton

1. Slavná minulost české hudby; kapitoly z dějin české hudby. 1959.

2. Jeremiáš, O. Praktické pokyny k instrumentaci symfonického orchestru. 1959.

3. ----. Praktické pokyny k dirigování. 1959.

4. Rychlík, J. Moderní instrumentace I. 1959.

5. Kulínský, B. Učíme se zpívat z not. 1963.

6. Stejskalová, M. U Janáčků, podle vyprávění Marie Stejskalové. At head of title: Marie Trkanová. 1959.

7. Bartoš, J. Z. Čtení o hudebních formách; populární přehled a zábavný výklad s notovými příklady a obrázky. 1960.

8. Očadlík, M. Vyprávění o Bedřichu Smetanovi. 1960.

9. Modr, A. Harmonie v otázkách a odpovědích. 2. přepracované vydání. 1960.

10. Slavná minulost německé hudby; kapitoly z dějin německé hudby. 1960.

11. Stašek, Č. Učíme se zpívat ve sboru. 1960.

12. Krautgartner, K. O instrumentaci tanečního a jazzového orchestru. 1961.

13. Horová, E. Nebojte se moderní hudby. 1961.

15. Gardavský, Č., et al. Skladatel dneška. 1961.

16. Očadlík, M. Svět orchestru; česká hudba. 3. přepracované vydání. 1962.

17. Slavná minulost ruské hudby. 1962.

18. Podešva, J. Současná hudba na západě. 1963.

Decca Music Guides
London: Cassell
1. Budden, L., ed. Beethoven; Symphonies. Part 1.
   1952.
2. ----. Beethoven; Symphonies. Part 2. 1952.
3. Stevens, H. C., ed. Brahms; Symphonies. 1952.
4. Mann, W., ed. Mozart; Symphonies. Part 1. 1952.
5. ----. Mozart; Symphonies. Part 2. 1952.
6. Dennes, M., ed. Beethoven; Concertos. 1952.
7. Amis, J., ed. Bach; Brandenburg Concertos. 1952.
8. Foss, H., ed. Mozart; Chamber Music. Part 1. 1952.
9. Neden, H., ed. Puccini; Operas. 1952.
10. Donington, R., ed. Stravinsky; Ballet Music. 1952.
11. Budden, R., ed. Tchaikovsky; Misc. Works. 1952.
12. Porter, A., ed. Richard Strauss; Tone Poems. 1952.

Detroit Studies in Music Bibliography. Ed. Bruno Nettl.
Detroit, Michigan: Information Service, Inc.
1. Nettl, B. Reference Materials in Ethnomusicology.
   1961.
2. Poladian, S. Sir Arthur Sullivan; An Index to the Texts
   of His Vocal Works. 1961.
3. MacArdle, D. W. An Index to Beethoven's Conversa-
   tion Books. 1962.
4. Mixter, K. W. General Bibliography for Music Research. 1962.
5. Mattfeld, J. A Handbook of American Operatic
   Premieres, 1731-1962. 1963.
6. Coover, J. B., & R. Colvig. Medieval and Renaissance Music on Long-Playing Records. 1964.
Mangler, J. E. Directory of Rhode Island Music and Musicians, 1733-1850. In prep.
MacArdle, D. W. The Periodical Literature of Beethoven's
   Chamber Music. In prep.

Documenta Musicologica. Faksimile-Reihe, hrsg. von der

71

Internationalen Gesellschaft für Musikwissenschaft und der Internationalen Vereinigung der Musikbibliotheken.

Kassel: Bärenreiter

Reihe 1: Druckschriften-Faksimiles

1. Rhau, G. Enchiridion utriusque musicae practicae (Musica plana). Wittenberg 1538. Hrsg. von Hans Albrecht. 1951.

2. Quantz, J. J. Versuch einer Anweisung, die flûte traversière zu spielen. 3. Auflage, Berlin 1789. Hrsg. von Hans-Peter Schmitz. 1953.

3. Walther, J. G. Musikalisches Lexikon, oder Musikalische Bibliothek. Leipzig 1732. Hrsg. von Richard Schaal. 1953.

4. Adlung, J. Anleitung zu der musikalischen Gelahrtheit (1758). Hrsg. von H. J. Moser. 1953.

5. Mattheson, J. Der vollkommene Capellmeister (1739). Hrsg. von Margarete Reimann. 1954.

6. Bourgeois, L. Le Droict Chemin de Musique (Genf, 1550). Hrsg. von André Gaillard. 1954.

7. L'Estocart, P. de. Cent cinquante Psaumes de David; mis en rime françoise par Clément Marot et Théodore de Bèsze, et mis en musique à quatre, cinq, six, sept et huit parties par Paschal de l'Estocart (1583). Hrsg. von Hanns Holliger und Pierre Pidoux. 1954. 5 part-books.

8. Majer, J. F. B. C. Museum musicum 1732. Hrsg. von Heinz Becker. 1954.

9. Coclico, A. P. Compendium musices. Hrsg. von Manfred F. Bukofzer. 1954.

10. Burmeister, J. Musica poetica (Rostock, 1606). Hrsg. von Martin Ruhnke. 1955.

11. Bermudo, J. Declaración de instrumentos musicales 1555. Hrsg. von Macario Santiago Kastner. 1957.

12. Bovicelli, G. B. Regole passaggi di musica 1594. Hrsg. von Nanie Bridgman. 1957.

13. Salinas, F. de. De musica. Hrsg. von Macario

Santiago Kastner. 1958.

14. Praetorius, M. Syntagma musicum. Hrsg. von
    Wilibald Gurlitt. Band 1: Musicae artis analecta. 1959.

15. ----. Band 2: De organographia. 1959. For Band 3,
    see No. 21 below.

16. Pontio, P. Ragionamento di musica (Parma 1588).
    Hrsg. von Suzanne Clercx. 1959.

17. Vicentino, N. L'antica musica ridotta alla moderna
    prattica. Hrsg. von Edward E. Lowinsky. 1959.

18. Adlung, J. Musica mechanica organoedi (Berlin, 1768).
    Hrsg. von Christhard Mahrenholz. 1961.

19. Burney, C. Tagebuch einer musikalischen Reise durch
    Frankreich, Italien, Flandern, die Niederlande und am
    Rhein bis Wien, durch Böhmen, Sachsen, Brandenburg,
    Hamburg, und Holland (1772/1773). Aus dem Englischen
    übersetzt von C. D. Eberling und J. J. C. Bode. Hrsg.
    von R. Schaal.

21. Praetorius, M. Syntagma musicum. Band 3: Termini
    musici. Hrsg. von W. Gurlitt. 1959. See also Bd. 14-15
    above.

22. Weigel, J. C. Musicalisches Theatrum. Hrsg. von
    Alfred Berner. 1961.

23. Türk, D. G. Klavierschule. 1. Ausgabe 1789. Hrsg.
    von E. R. Jacobi. 1962.

24-26 Bedos de Celles, Dom F. L'Art du facteur d'orgues.
    Hrsg. von C. Mahrenholz. 4 Bände in 3. 1963.

Reihe 2: Handschriften-Faksimiles. Outside the scope of this
study.

Documents sur la musique
Paris: Richard Masse

2. Adrian, P. G. Rêflexions sur l'univers sonore; essai sur
   la musique. 1955. Ceased publication. The publisher can-
   not supply information about Vol. 1.

Drucke zur Münchner Musikgeschichte

München: Musikantiquariat Ricke
1. Kende, G. K. Richard Strauss und Clemens Krauss; eine Künstlerfreundschaft und ihre Zusammenarbeit an "Capriccio" (op. 85), Konversationsstück für Musik. 1960.
2. Scanzoni, S. von. Richard Strauss und seine Sänger. 1961.
3. Ott, A. Richard Trunk; Leben und Werk. 1964.

Edícia hudobnej literatúry
Bratislava: SVKL, SHV (25?-)
15. Schneider-Trnavský, M. Úsmevy a slzy; spomienky trnavského skladatela. 1959.
20. Rolland, R. Hudobníci pritomnosti. 1960.
22. Šimůnek, E. Estetika rozvoja súčasnej hudby. 1960.
23. Pražák, P. Osobnosti českej hudby I. 1961.
24. Searle, H. Hudba F. Liszta. Přel. Lydia Lenhardtová. 1961.
25. Pražák, P. Osobnosti českej hudby II. 1962.
26. Kunin, J. F. Peter Iljič Čajkovskij. Přel. Nina Vietorová. 1962.
26. Szabolcsi, B. Dějiny hudby. Přel. Julius Albrecht. 1962.
According to SHV, two vols. appeared with number "26."
27. Werfel, F. Verdi. Přel. Štefan Hovarth. 1963.
28. Nejgauz, G. G. Poetika klavíra. Z rus. orig. Přel. Zora Jesenská. 1963.

Erlanger Arbeiten zur Musikwissenschaft. Hrsg. von Bruno Stäblein.
München: W. Ricke
1. Thannabaur, P. J. Das einstimmige Sanctus der römischen Messe in der handschriftlichen Ueberlieferung des 11. bis 16. Jahrhunderts. 1962.
Lang, A. Die musikalische Ueberlieferung des provenzalischen Minnesangs; Quellen und Repertoire. In prep.
Stäblein, B., & T. Wohnhaas, ed. Strophenan-

74

fänge der gesungenen lateinischen geistlichen Dichtung des Mittelalters (nach den Analecta Hymnica). I. Teil: Sequenzen. In prep.
Further vols. (dealing with the repertory of tropes, alleluias, and offices) in prep.

Ethno-Musicologica. Ed. by S. Baud-Bovy, C. Brailoiu, J. Kunst, W. Wiora.
Leiden: E. J. Brill
1. Kunst, J. Metre, Rhythm, Multi-Part Music. 1950. Also in French and Flemish editions.
2. Husmann, H. Fünf- und siebenstellige Centstafeln zur Berechnung musikalischer Intervalle. 1951.
3. Harich-Schneider, E. The Rhythmical Patterns in Gagaku und Bugaku. 1954.

Évocations des Jeunesses Musicales de Belgique
Bruxelles: Édition des Jeunesses Musicales
1. Nys, P. L'apothéose de Haendel; évocation musicale en six tableaux. 1949.
2. ----. Beethoven; évocation musicale et dramatique en dix tableaux. 1950.

Fachbuchreihe Das Musikinstrument
Frankfurt am Main: Verlag Das Musikinstrument
1. Arakélian, S. Die Geige; Ratschläge und Anmerkungen eines Geigenbauers.
2. Funke, O. Das Klavier und seine Pflege; Theorie und Praxis des Klavierstimmens. 3. Auflage 1958.
3. Fenner, K. Bestimmung der Saitenspannung des Pianos; Arbeitshilfe zur Bestimmung sämtlicher Saitenspannungen. Längen und Stärken bei Blankbezug. 1959. Bearb. von H. K. Herzog. Complete text in German, Eng., Fr., Spanish and It. editions. See Schriftenreihe Das Musikinstrument, Heft 3, for supplement.
4. Junghanns, H., et al. Der Piano- und Flügelbau. 3. Auflage 1960.

5. Funke, O. Le piano; son entretien et son accord. Trad. par P. Meyer-Siat. 1961.

6. ----. The Piano and How to Care For It; Piano Tuning in Theory and Practice. Trans. by Roy Wisbey and C.H. Wehlau. 1961.

7. Nix, J. Lehrgang der Stimmkunst. 1961.

8. Rödig, H. Geigenbau in neuer Sicht; neue Erkenntnisse über das Wesen der Resonanz in Streichinstrumenten. 1962.

9. Pfeiffer, W. Vom Hammer; Untersuchungen aus einem Teilgebiet des Flügel- und Klavierbaues. Faksimile-Druck. 1962.

10. Berr, A. Geigen; Originale, Kopien, Fälschungen, Verfälschungen. 1962.

Faksimile-Reihe Bachscher Werke und Schriftstücke. Hrsg. vom Bach-Archiv, Leipzig.
Leipzig: Deutscher Verlag für Musik (Kassel: Bärenreiter)

1. Bach, J.S. Kurtzer, iedoch höchstnöthiger Entwurff einer wohlbestallten Kirchen Music; nebst einigen unvorgreiflichen Bedencken von dem Verfall derselben. Leipzig, den 23 Aug. 1730. Faksimile der Handschrift, mit Nachwort von Werner Neumann. 1955.

2. ----. Originalstimmensatz der Kantate "Wär Gott nicht mit uns diese Zeit" (BWV 14). Mit Vorwort von Werner Neumann. 1955.

3. ----. Brief an den Jugendfreund Georg Erdmann vom 28. Oktober 1730. Mit Nachwort von N. Notowicz. 1960.

4. ----. Sonata h-Moll (BWV 1030). Mit Nachwort von Werner Neumann. 1961.

5. ----. Das wohltemperierte Clavier (BWV 846-893). 1. Vorwort von H. Pischner, 2. Vorwort von K.-H. Köhler. Teil 1. 1962.

The Field of Music Series. Ed. by Ernest Hutcheson.
N.Y., Toronto: Rinehart

1. Goldman, R. F. The Concert Band. 1946.
2. Letz, H. Music for the Violin and Viola. 1948.
3. Kagen, S. Music for the Voice; A Descriptive List of
Concert and Teaching Material. 1949.
4. ----. On Studying Singing. 1950.
5. Friskin, J., & I. Freundlich. Music for the Piano;
A Handbook of Concert and Teaching Material from
1580 to 1952. 1954.

Folkeuniversitetets bibliotek. Musik. Udgivet af Folkeuniversitetsforeningen i København.
København: Rhodos
1. Hamburger, P. Tjajkovskij som symfoniker. 1962.
2. Balzer, J. Béla Bartók; en portraetskitse. 1962.

Forschungsbeiträge zur Musikwissenschaft
Regensburg: G. Bosse
1. Melnicki, M. Das einstimmige Kyrie des lateinischen
Mittelalters. 1955.
2. Bosse, D. Untersuchungen einstimmiger mittelalter-
licher Melodien zum "Gloria in excelsis deo." 1955.
3. Traimer, Roswitha. Béla Bartóks Kompositionstechnik,
dargestellt an seinen sechs Streichquartetten. 1956.
4. Stephani, H. Zur Psychologie des musikalischen Hörens.
1956.
5. Kiekert, I. Die musikalische Form in den Werken
Carl Orff's. 1957.
6. Lindlar, H. Igor Strawinskys sakraler Gesang; Geist
und Form der christ-kultischen Kompositionen. 1957.
7. Mayerhofer, G. "Abermals vom Freischützen"; der
Münchner "Freischütze" von 1812. 1959.
8. Scharschuch, H. Analyse zu Igor Strawinsky's "Sacre
du printemps." 1960.
9. Seifert, W. Christian Gottfried Körner; ein Musikästhe-
tiker der deutschen Klassik. 1960.
10. Bitter, C. Wandlungen in den Inszenierungsformen des

"Don Giovanni" von 1787 bis 1928; zur Problematik des musikalischen Theaters in Deutschland. 1961.

11. Rohlfs, E. Die deutschsprachigen Musikperiodica 1945-1957. 1961.

12. Scharschuch, H. Gesamtanalyse der Harmonik von Richard Wagners Musikdrama "Tristan und Isolde" unter spezieller Berücksichtigung der Sequenztechnik des Tristanstiles. 1963.

13. Marx, K. Die Entwicklung des Violoncells und seiner Spieltechnik bis J. L. Duport, 1520-1820. 1963.

Fountain Music Series. Ed. by the Rural Music Schools Association.

London: Fountain Press

1. Bruxner, M. An Ear for Music. 1953.

2. Shaw, H. W. How to Read Music. 1953.

3. Harris, R. J. , & E. Palmer. How to Choose an Instrument; Piano and Strings. 1953.

4. Camden, A. J. Kerrison. How to Choose an Instrument; Woodwind and Brass. 1953.

5. Noble, R. , et al. How to Choose an Instrument; Recorders, Percussion, Saxophones. 1954.

Freiburger Studien zur Musikwissenschaft. 2. Reihe der Veröffentlichungen des Musikwissenschaftlichen Instituts der Universität Freiburg i. d.   Schweiz.

Regensburg: F. Pustet; Freiburg: Universitätsverlag (Bd. 6 $\not$)

1. Domp, J. Studien zur Geschichte der Musik an westfälischen Adelshöfen im XVIII. Jahrhundert. 1934.

2. Hieronymus de Moravia. Tractatus de musica. 1935.

3. Fellerer, K. G. Mittelalterliches Musikleben der Stadt Freiburg im Uechtland. 1935.

4. Amann, J. Allegris Miserere und die Aufführungspraxis in der Sixtina nach Reiseberichten und Musikhandschriften. 1935.

5. Bösken, F.   Musikgeschichte der Stadt Osnabrück;

die geistliche und weltliche Musik bis zum Beginne des
19. Jahrhunderts. 1937.
6. Jerger, W. Constantin Reindl, 1738-1799; ein Beitrag
zur Musikgeschichte der deutschen Schweiz im 18.
Jahrhundert. 1955.
7. ----. Die Haydndrucke aus dem Archiv der Theater- und
Musik-Liebhabergesellschaft zu Luzern, nebst Materialien
zum Musikleben in Luzern um 1800. 1959.

Göttinger musikwissenschaftliche Arbeiten. Hrsg. von
Hermann Zenck.
Kassel: Bärenreiter
1. Luther, W. M. Gallus Dressler; ein Beitrag zur Ge-
schichte des Protestantischen Schulkantorats im 16.
Jahrhundert. Preface 1941. 1945.

Gottmer muziek pockets
Haarlem: Gottmer
1. Loeser, N. Chopin. 1958.
2. Wagemans. H. Schubert. 1958.
3. Kuringer, P. Johann Strauss. 1958. 3. druk 1961.
4. Muller, H. J. M. Tsjaikofsky. 1958.
5. Loeser, N. Beethoven. 1958. 2. druk 1961.
6. Rutters, H. Handel. 1958.
7. Douliez, P. Debussy. 1958.
8. Monnikendam, M. Strawinsky. 1958.
9. Geraedts, H. , & J. Geraedts. Béla Bartôk. 1958.
   2. druk 1961.
10. Cuypers, J. Grieg. 1959.
11. Verbeke, R. Berlioz. 1959.
12. Koole, A. Mendelssohn. 1959.
13. Geraedts, J. Ravel. 1959.
14. Berkel, C. van. Rossini. 1959.
15. Kat, A. I. M. Palestrina. 1959.
16. Ravenzwaaij, G. van. Purcell. 1959.
17. Stam, H. Schumann. 1959.

18. Hengel, W. van. Bruckner. 1959.
19. Loeser, N. Wolf. 1959.
20. Prick van Wely, M. Dvořák. 1959.
21. Loeser, N. Mahler. 1960.
22. Schouwman, H. Sibelius. 1960.
23. Loeser, N. Moussorgsky. 1960.
24. Douliez, P. Benoit. 1960.
25. Doorninck, M. van. Puccini. 1960.
26. Thysse, W. H. Haydn. 2. druk. 1959.
27. Loeser, N. Mozart. 3. druk 1959. 4. druk 1961.
28. ----. Vivaldi. 1959.
29. Brandts Buys, H. Bach. 1960.
30. Pahlen, K.   Manuel de Falla. 1961.
No further vols. currently in prep.

I Grandi musicisti
Modena, Parma: U. Guanda
1. Valabrega, C. Giovanni Sebastiano Bach. 1950.
2. ----. Schumann; arte e natura, arte e vita, arte e
   fede. 1934. 2a ed. 1950.
Continued under the title: Biblioteca di cultura musicale.

Les Grands compositeurs du XXe siècle. Collection dirigée
   par Bernard Gavoty.
Genève: Éditions René Kister
1. Vuillermoz, É.   Claude Debussy. 1957.
2. Pincherle, M. Albert Roussel. 1957.
No others appeared. German ed.: Grossen Komponisten
   des 20. Jahrhunderts.

Les Grands musiciens. Collection dirigée par Jean Witold.
Paris: Éditions du Coudrier
1. Chailley, J. La musique médiévale. Préface de Gustave Cohen. 1951.
2. Le Roux, M. Claudio Monteverdi. Préface de Roland-
   Manuel. 1951.

3. Fischer, E. Considérations sur la musique. Traduit
   de l'allemand par Charles-Marie de Boncourt. 1951.

Die grossen Komponisten des 20. Jahrhunderts. Unter der
   Leitung von Bernard Gavoty.
Genève: Éditions René Kister
1. Vuillermoz, E. Claude Debussy. 1957.
2. Pincherle, A. Albert Roussel. 1957.
No others appeared. French ed.: Les Grands compositeurs
   du XXe siècle.

Guide musicali
Firenze: Casa Editrice Monsalvato; F. Fussi (1946-)
1. Guerrini, G., & P. Fragapane. Il dottor Faust di
   Ferruccio Busoni. 1942.
2. Luciani, S. A. Il Tristano e Isolda di Riccardo Wagner.
   1942.
3. Marini, R. B. La Turandot di Giacomo Puccini. 1942.
4. Rinaldi, M.   Il Falstaff di G. Verdi. 1942.
5. ----. Lo Straniero di I. Pizzetti. 1943.
6. Damerini, A. La Kovanstchina di M. Mussorgskij.
   1943.
7. Bonaccorsi, A. La musica popolare. 1943.
8. Rinaldi, M. L'Aida di G. Verdi. 1943.
9. Damerini, A. L'Oro del Reno di R. Wagner. 1944.
10. Paoli, R. La Walkiria di R. Wagner. 1944.
11. Gavazzeni, G. Il Siegfried di R. Wagner. 1944.
12. Hermet, A. Il Crepuscolo degli Dei di R. Wagner.
   1944.
13. Labroca, M. Il Flauto Magico di W. A. Mozart. 1944.
14. Roncaglia, G. L'Otello di Giuseppe Verdi. 1946.
15. Damerini, A. Salomè di Riccardo Strauss. 1948.

Guide musicali dell'Istituto d'Alta Cultura
Milano: Istituto d'Alta Cultura
1. Rinaldi, M. Elettra di R. Strauss.

2. Corte, A. della. Rigoletto, Il Trovatore, La Traviata di G. Verdi.

3. Rinaldi, M. La Fanciulla del West di G. Puccini.

4. Corte, A. della. Rigoletto, Il Trovatore, La Traviata, Aida, Otello, Falstaff; le sei più belle opere di Giuseppe Verdi. 1946.

5. Gavazzeni, G. L'Oro di I. Pizzetti. 1946.

6. Confalonieri, G. Gioacchino Rossini; Cenerentola. 1946.

7. Abbiati, F. Benjamin Britten; Peter Grimes. 1946.

8. Malipiero, R. Maurice Ravel; L'Enfant et les sortilèges, La Valse, Daphnis et Chloê. 1948.

9. Chailly, L. Domenico Cimarosa; Il matrimonio segreto. 1949.

10. Malipiero, R. Claude Debussy; Pelléas et Mélisande. 1949.

12. Mila, M. Igor Strawinsky; Carriera d'un libertino (The Rake's Progress). 1951.

Hesses Handbücher der Musik
Berlin: Max Hesses Verlag
Volumes issued or reissued since 1950:

2/3. Moser, H. J. Lehrbuch der Musikgeschichte. 1936. 11. durchges. und verm. Auflage 1950. 12. neubearb. Auflage 1963.

15&25. Grabner, H. Handbuch der Harmonielehre. Teil I: Lehrbuch. Teil II: Aufgabenbuch. 3. Auflage 1955.

76. Busoni, F. Wesen und Einheit der Musik. Neuausgabe der Schriften und Aufzeichnungen Busonis, revidiert und erg. von Joachim Herrmann. 1956.

100. Grabner, H. Neue Gehörübung. 1950.

101. Döbereiner, C. Zur Renaissance alter Musik. 1950.

102. Altmann, W. Kleine Führer durch die Streichquartette für Haus und Schule. 1950.

103. Müller-Blattau, J. M. Taschenlexikon der Fremd- und Fachwörter der Musik.

104. Epping, A. ABC der Improvisation; mit Aufgaben zum Singen und Spielen. 1954.
105. Jakobi, T. Die Kunst des Partiturspielens. 1956.
106. Grabner, H. Die Kunst des Orgelbaues. 1958.
107. Sauer, W. Beethoven und das Wesen der Musik. 1958.
108. Kickton, E. Musikwissenschaft im Umriss. 1958.
109. Singer, K. Die Berufskrankheiten der Musiker; systematische Darstellungen ihrer Ursachen, Symptome und Behandlungsmethoden. 2. Auflage, neu bearb. von A. Salomon. Vorwort von Fritz Winckel. 1960.

Hesses kleine Bücherei
Berlin: Max Hesses Verlag
 1. Stuckenschmidt, H. H. Glanz und Elend der Musikkritik; der Verfall des musikalischen Geschmacks. 1957.
 2. Offenbach, J. Offenbach in Amerika; Reisenotizen eines Musikers. Uebers. und eingeleitet von Reinhold Scharnke. 1957.
 3. Komorzyński, E. von. Pamina; Mozarts letzte Liebe. 1957.
 4. Longolius, C. George Gershwin. 1959.
 5. Vogelsang, K. Alban Berg; Leben und Werk. 1959.
 6. Worbs, H. C. Gustav Mahler. 1960.

Hinrichsen's Facsimile Reprints
London: Hinrichsen. Partly titled: Facsimile Reprint; partly numbered.
 1. Wesley, S. S. Letters of Samuel Wesley to Mr. Jacobs, Organist of Surrey Chapel, relating to the introduction into this country of the works of John Sebastian Bach. Ed. by his daughter Eliza Wesley. Cover title: Samuel Wesley's Famous Bach Letters. 1957.
 2. ----. A Few Words on Cathedral Music. Reprint of the original edition of 24th May 1849, with an Intro. by Rev. W. Francis Westbrook and some historical notes by Gerald W. Spink (the biographer of S. S. Wesley).

1961.

3. Playford, J. Musick's Recreation on "The Viol, Lyra-way." Intro. by Nathalie Dolmetsch. 1960.

Hinrichsen's Miniature Surveys
London: Hinrichsen

1. Gundry, I. Opera in a Nutshell. Preface by Edward J. Dent. 1945.

2. Shaw, H. W. Handel's Messiah; The Story of a Master-piece. 1946.

3. Parry, W. H. Thirteen Centuries of English Church Music; Introduction to a Great National Tradition. 1946. 2nd enlarged ed. 1947.

4. Shaw, H. W. Beethoven's Fifth Piano Concerto (The Emperor); A Guide. 1947.

5. Gundry, I. Men of the Hills; Introduction to a New English Opera, "The Partisans," written and composed by Inglis Gundry. Foreword by Rutland Boughton, includ-ing also "A Note on 'The Partisans' " by Geoffrey Cor-bett; "The Traditional Guerilla Songs of the Balkans," by A. L. Lloyd; and "The Dances" by Joan Lawson. 1948.

6. Did not appear.

7. Anderson, W. R. Rachmaninov and His Concertos; A Brief Sketch of the Composer and His Style. 1948.

8-13 Did not appear.

14. Ellingford, H. F. Masonic Music in England; A Histori-cal Survey. 1949.

15. Bergmann, W. G. , et al. Practical Music for All, by W. G. Bergmann, K. Blocksidge, M. E. Calthrop, F. Green, I. Gundry, H. C. Hind, J. McN. Milne, J. R. Tobin. Intro. by Christopher le Fleming; Conclusion by H. Watkins Shaw. 1952.

16a. Langwill, L. G. , H. C. Hind, & R. Morley-Pegge. Waits, Wind Band, Horn. Intro. by Max Hinrichsen. 1952.

16b. Greig, J.R. Grieg and His Scottish Ancestry. With "A Concise Grieg Bibliography" by Max Hinrichsen. 1952.

17. Cook, K. Oh, Listen to the Band; A Miscellany compiled and edited by Kenneth Cook. Intro. by Henry Geehl. 1950.

18. Williams, S. Verdi's Last Operas: Aida, Othello, Falstaff. 1951.

19. Culshaw, J. Brahms; An Outline of His Life and Music. Preface by Alec Robertson. 1952.

20. Beethoven, L. van.   Beethoven's Own Words, compiled and annotated by Philip Kruseman, trans. by Herbert Antcliffe. 1948.

21. Hannikainen, I. Sibelius and the Development of Finnish Music. Preface by Toivo Hapaanen. 1952.

22. Cook, K. The Bandman's Everything Within. Foreword by Denis Wright. 1951.

23. Civic Entertainment and Its Cost; A Survey of the Activities of the Local Authorities in Greater London. Foreword by Sir Kenneth Barnes, Preface by Professor W.A. Robson, and Essays by the Chairmen of the two Arts Committees of the House of Commons, Dr. Barnett Stross, M.P., and Hamilton Kerr, M.P. 1956.

24. Langwill, L.G. Bassoon and Double Bassoon; A Short Illustrated History of Their Origin, Development and Makers. 1951.

25. Stocks, H.C.L. British Cathedral Organists. 1950.

"Historiae musicae cultores" biblioteca
Firenze: L.S. Olschki

1. Gabinetto disegni e stampe degli Uffizi. Mostra di strumenti musicali in disegni degli Uffizi. Catalogo a cura di Luisa Marcucci, con pref. di Luigi Parigi. 1952.

2. Collectanea historiae musicae, Vol. 1. 1953.

3. Parigi, L. "Laurentiana"; Lorenzo dei Medici cultore

della musica. 1954.

4. Briganti, F. Gio. Andrea Angelini-Bontempi (1624-1705); musicista, letterato, architetto. 1956.

5. Roncaglia, G. La Cappella musicale del Duomo di Modena. 1957.

6. Collectanea historiae musicae, Vol. 2. 1956.

7. Paccagnella, E. Palestrina; il linguaggio melodico e armonico. 1957.

8. Carrara, M. La Intavolatura di liuto, 1585. A cura di Benvenuto Disertori. 1957.

9. Tiby, O. Il Real Teatro carolino e l'ottocento musicale palermitano. 1957.

10. Lunelli, R. L'arte organaria del rinascimento in Roma e gli organi di S. Pietro in Vaticano dalle origini a tutto il periodo frescobaldiano. 1958.

11. Ricci des Ferres-Cancani, G. Francesco Morlacchi (1784-1841); un maestro italiano alla corte di Sassonia. 1958.

12. Allorto, R. Le sonate per pianoforte di Muzio Clementi; studio critico e catalogo tematico. 1959.

13. Gallico, C. Un canzoniere musicale italiano del cinquecento (Bologna, Cons. Mus. Ms. Q 21). 1961.

14. Anselmo, G. De musica. Introduzione, testo e commento a cura di Giuseppe Massera. 1961.

15. Gamberini, L. La parola e la musica nell'antichità; confronto fra documenti musicali antichi e dei primi secoli del medio evo. 1962.

16. Fabbri, M. Alessandro Scarlatti e il Principe Ferdinando de'Medici. 1961.

17. Collectanea historiae musicae, Vol. 3. 1963.

18. Franciscus de Brugis. Ad cantores Prefatio et Opusculum una cum manu perfecta. A cura di Giuseppe Massera. 1963.

19. Luigi Cherubini nel II centenario della nascita; contributo alla conoscenza della vita e dell'opera. 1962.

20. Fabbri, M. Francesco Corteccia e la Firenze musicale

del suo tempo. In prep.

Hudba na každém kroku. Řídí Jiří Pilka a Jaroslav Smolka.
Praha: SNKLHU (1-5), SHV (6-)
1. Pilka, J. Setkání s hudbou. 1960.
2. Šíp, L. Pěvci před mikrofonem. 1960.
3. Šrom, K. Orchestr a dirigent. 1960.
4. Mlejnek, K. O valčíku a jeho tvůrcích. 1960.
5. Pospíšil, V. S českou filharmonií třemi světadíly. 1960.
6. Lébl, V. Cesty moderní opery. 1961.
7. Poledňák, I. Kapitolky o jazzu. 1961.
8. Smolka, J. Česká hudba našeho století. 1961.
9. Šíp, Ladislav. Nahrávání a reprodukovaná hudba. 1961.
10. Pospíšil, V. Slavní hosté Pražských jar. 1962.
11. Mlejnek, K. Smetanovci, Janáčkovci a Vlachovci. 1962.
12. Kučera, V. Talent, mistrovství, světový názor. 1962.
13. Břešťák, V. Poznáváme komorní hudbu. 1963.
14. Nedbal, K. , & V. Pospíšil. Slavní světoví dirigenti.
    1963.
15. Burghauser, J. Slavní čeští dirigenti. 1963.
16. Barvík, M. Hudba revolucí. 1964.
17. Bek, J. Impresionismus a hudba. 1964.

Hudebně-pedagogická knihovna Rovnosti
Brno: Nakladatelství Rovnost v Brně
1. Blažek, Z. Dvojsměrná alterace v harmonickém
   myšlení. 1949.

Hudební Edice SSÚ [Slezského studijního ustavu]
Ostrava: Krajské nakladatelství
10. Stolařík, I. , ed. Jan Löwenbach a Leoš Janáček;
    vzájemná korespondence. 1958.
11. ----. Leoš Janáček; Ostravsko k 30. výročí úmrti;
    sborník vzpomínek. 1958.
13. Racek, J. Neznámá Mozartova autografní torsa. 1959.

Hudební knihovna Rovnosti. Řídí Jan Racek.

Brno: Rovnost

3/4. Barvík, M. O problému estetického hodnocení hudby. [Also] : Antonín Sychra. K otázce funkce současné opery. 1948. (=Práce a referáty z Hudebně-vědeckého semináře Filosofické fakulty Masarykovy university v Brně. Studijní rok 1946/47, číslo 3-4).

Hudební příručky pro každého

Brno: Pazdírkovo Nakladatelství

1. Barvík, M. Chci umět modulovat. 1947.

Hudební profily. Edici řídí Věra Dolanská.

Praha: SNKLHU, later SHV

1. Berkovec, J. Josef Suk. 1956. 2. vyd. 1962.
2. Klíma, S. V. Josef Slavík. 1956.
3. Bachtík, J. Edvard Grieg. 1957.
4. Iwaszkiewicz, J. Frederyk Chopin. 1957. 2. vyd. 1958.
5. Karásek, B. Wolfgang Amadeus Mozart. 1959.
6. Holzknecht, V. Claude Debussy. 1958.
7. Sietz, R. Henry Purcell. 1960.
8. Šeda, J. Leoš Janáček. 1961.
9. Pálová-Vrbová, Z. Béla Bartók. 1963.
10. Jiránek, Jaroslav. Zdeněk Fibich. 1963.
11. Bachtík, J. Giuseppe Verdi. 1963.
12. Burian, K. V. Giocchimo Rossini. 1963.

Hudební rozpravy. Řídí Eduard Herzog.

Praha: SNKLHU (1-8), SHV (9-)

1. Zich, J. Instrumentace Smetanova Dalibora; esteticko-theoretická studie. 1957.
2. Berkovec, J. Jiráskův F. L. Věk--skladatel; hudební portrét F. V. Heka. 1958.
3. Risinger, K. Základní harmonické funkce v soudobé hudbě. 1958.

4. Zich, J. Prostředky výkonného hudebního umění. 1959.
5. Burghauser, J. Orchestrace Dvořákových Slovanských tanců. 1959.
6. Mihule, J.   Symfonie Bohuslava Martinů. 1959.
7. Rychlík, J. Žestové nástroje bez strojiva. 1960.
8. Pilková, Z. Dramatická tvorba Jiřího Bendy. 1960.
9. Poštolka, M. Joseph Haydn a naše hudba 18. století; úvod do problematiky vzájemných vztahů. 1961.
10. Kohoutek, C. Novodobé skladebné teorie západoevropské hudby. 1962.
11. Risinger, K. Vůdčí osobnosti české moderní hudební teorie; Otakar Šín, Alois Hába,   Karel Janeček. 1963.

Hudobné profily
Bratislava: SHV
1. Zavarsky, E. Maurice Ravel. 1963.

Institutt for Musikkvitenskap, Universitetet i Oslo. Skrifter.
Oslo: Universitetsforlaget
1. Benestad, F. Johannes Haarklou; mannen og verket. 1961.
2. ----. Waldemar Thrane, en pionér i norsk musikkliv. 1961.
3. Schjelderup-Ebbe, D.   Purcell's Cadences. 1962.
4. Gurvin, O. Fartein Valen; en banebryter i nyere norsk musikk. Drammen & Oslo: H. Lyche, 1962.

International Music Council. Publications.
Paris: UNESCO House
1. International Music Council. Foundation, First and Second General Assemblies, Statutes, Rules of Procedure, Programme, Members, Delegates, Commissions. 1951.

Janáčkův archiv. Vydává filosofická fakulta Masarykovy University v Brně. Řídí Jan Racek.

Praha: Hudební Matice Umělecké Besedy (1-7), Orbis (18),
SNKLHU (9- & Řada 2)
Řada 1
1. Korespondence Leoše Janáčka s Artušem Rektorysem.
Rozebráno. Viz sv. 4.
2. Korespondence Leoše Janáčka s Otakarem Ostrčilem. K
tisku připravil A. Rektorys.
3. Korrespondence Leoše Janáčka s F. S. Procházkou. K
tisku připravil A. Rektorys.
4. Korespondence Leoše Janáčka s Artušem Rektorysem.
Vydal Artuš Rektorys. 2. vyd. rozšířené o 21 dopisů
L. J. a o dopisy A. Rektoryse L. Janáčkovi. 1949.
5. Korespondence Leoše Janáčka s libretisty Výletů Broučko-
vých. K tisku připravil Artuš Rektorys.
6. Korespondence Leoše Janáčka s Gabrielou Horvátovou.
Vydal Artuš Rektorys.
7. Korespondence Leoše Janáčka s Karlem Kovařovicem. K
tisku připravil Artuš Rektorys. 1950.
8. Korespondence Leoše Janáčka s Marií Calmou a
Dr. Františkem Veselým. Vydali Jan Racek a Artuš
Rektorys. 1951.
9. Korespondence Leoše Janáčka s Maxem Brodem. Vydali
Jan Racek a Artuš Rektorys. 1953.

Řada 2
1. Janáček, L. O lidové písni a lidové hudbě; dokumenty a
studie. K vyd. připravil a poznámkami opatřil Jiří Vysloužil. 1955.

Jazz
Stockholm: Hörsta
1. Lambert, G. E. Duke Ellington. Oevers. L. Anderson.
1959.
2. Oliver, P. Bessie Smith. Oevers. Bo Holmqvist. 1959.
3. James, M. Dizzy Gillespie. Oevers. C.-E. Lindgren.
1959.
4. James, B. Bix Beiderbecke. Oevers. S. Foerster.

1959.

Jazz-Bücherei; Lebensbeschreibungen für alle Freunde der
   Jazz. Hrsg. von Hans Heinrich Reinfeldt.
Wetzlar: Pegasus Verlag
1. Kunst, P. Sidney Bechet. 1959.
2. Burkhardt, W., & J. Gerth. Lester Young. 1959.
3. Schmidt, S. Charlie Parker. 1959.
4. Jungermann, J. Ella Fitzgerald. 1960.
5. Lange, H. H. Loring "Red" Nichols. 1960.
6. Schulz-Köhn, D. Django Reinhardt. 1960.
7. Götze, W. Dizzy Gillespie. 1960.
8. Lange, H. H. Nick Larocca. 1960.
9. Schulz-Köhn, D. Stan Kenton. 1961.
10. Wachler, I. Benny Goodman. 1961.
11. Kayser, E. Mahalia Jackson. 1962.
12. Winkler, H. J.   Louis Armstrong. 1962.

Jazz Monographs
Stanhope, N. J.: Walter C. Allen
1. Allen, W. C., & B. A. L. Rust. King Joe Oliver.
   Belleville, N. J., 1955. Reprinted in Eng. for the Jazz
   Book Club, and again by Sidgwick & Jackson Ltd.
2. Charters, S. B. Jazz; New Orleans, 1885-1957. An
   Index to the Negro Musicians of New Orleans. 1958.
3. Waters, H. J. Jack Teagarden's Music; His Career and
   Recordings. Foreword by Paul Whiteman. 1960.

Jazz Publications
Basel: Jazz Publications
1. Wyler, M. A Glimpse at the Past; An Illustrated
   History of Some Early Record Companies That Made
   Jazz History. 1957.
2. Discography of Lionel Hampton & His Orchestra,
   1951-53. 1961.
4. Demeusy, B., & O. Flückiger. Arnett Cobb. 1962.

5. Demeusy, B. , & O. Flückiger. Discography of Lucky Millinder. 1962.

6. ----. Discography of Lionel Hampton, 1954-58. 1962.

Jenaer Beiträge zur Musikforschung. Hrsg. von Heinrich Besseler.

Leipzig: Breitkopf & Härtel

1. Hoffmann-Erbrecht, L. Deutsche und italienische Klaviermusik zur Bachzeit; Studien zur Thematik und Themenverarbeitung in der Zeit von 1720-1760. 1954.

2. Walther, J. G. Praecepta der musicalischen Composition, hrsg. von Peter Benary. 1955.

3. Benary, P. Die deutsche Kompositionslehre des 18. Jahrhunderts. Compendium Musices von Johann Adolph Scheibe als Erstdruck im Anhang. 1961.

Kantelenreeks

Utrecht: De Torentrans

1. Loeser, N. Rossini en zijn Barbier van Sevilla. 1952?

Keystone Books in Music

Philadelphia: Lippincott. 9 titles among other Keystone Books; further titles not anticipated.

3. Broder, N. The Collector's Bach. 1958.

4. Wilson, J. S. The Collector's Jazz; Traditional and Swing. 1958.

7. Burke, C. G. The Collector's Haydn. 1959.

8. Schonberg, H. C. The Collector's Chopin and Schumann. 1959.

9. Briggs, J. The Collector's Tchaikovsky and the Five. 1959.

10. Wilson, J. S. The Collector's Jazz; Modern. 1959.

23. Cohn, A. The Collector's Twentieth-Century Music in the Western Hemisphere. 1961.

Briggs, J. The Collector's Beethoven. 1962.

De Schauensee, M. The Collector's Verdi and Puccini.

1962.

Kings of Jazz
London: Cassell
1. Lambert, G. E. Duke Ellington. 1959.
2. James, M. Dizzy Gillespie. 1959.
3. Oliver, P. Bessie Smith. 1959.
4. James, B. Bix Beiderbecke. 1959.
5. McCarthy, A. J. Louis Armstrong. 1960.
6. Harrison, M. Charlie Parker. 1960.
7. Fox, C. Fats Waller. 1960.
8. Williams, M. King Oliver. 1960.
9. James, M. Miles Davis. 1961.
10. Lambert, G. E. Johnny Dodds. 1961.
11. Williams, M. Jelly Roll Morton. 1962.

Kings of Jazz
Teufen: Verlag Arthur Niggli
1. Armstrong, L. Louis Armstrong. 1961.
2. Williams, M.   King Oliver. 1961.
3. James, M. Dizzy Gillespie. 1961.
4. Oliver, P. Bessie Smith. 1961.

Kinnor. Dirigée par l'Association Saint Ambroise Pour le
   Chant Sacré du Peuple.
Paris: Éditions Fleurus
Série études
1. Gelineau, J. Chant et musique dans le culte chrétien;
   principes, lois et applications. 1962.
2. Deiss, L. Les acclamations liturgiques. In prep.
3. Labat, Sister E. P.   Essai sur le mystère
   de la musique. 1963.
4. Rivière, M.-A. Études sur l'antiphonaire de l'office. In
   prep.
Série documents. In prep.
   Kaelin, P. Pour bien chanter.

Klotz, H. Le livre de l'orgue. Traduit de l'allemand par
R. Reboud.

Julien, D. Pour faire chanter ma paroisse.

Rivière, M.-A. Antiennes brèves grégoriennes.

Nassoy, G. Le guide liturgique de l'organiste.

Kis zenei könyvtár
Budapest: Bibliotheca (1-4), Gondolat (5-)
1. Rolland, R. Ludwig van Beethoven. 1958.
2. Sólyom, G. Joseph Haydn. 1958.
3. Jemnitz, S.   Felix Mendelssohn Bartholdy. 1958.
4. Kroó, G. Robert Schumann. 1958.
5. Molnár, A. Johannes Brahms. 1959.
7. Ujfalussy, J. Achille-Claude Debussy. 1959.
8. Petrovics, E. Maurice Ravel. 1959.
8. Várnai, P. Heinrich Schütz. 1959.
The above two vols. are numbered "8"; undoubtedly in one
case this is a misprint for "6".
9. Pernye, A. Giacomo Puccini. 1959.
10. Kárpáti, J. Domenico Scarlatti. 1959.
11. Legány, D. Henry Purcell. 1959.
12. Rolland, R. Jean-Baptiste Lully. 1959.
13. Bartha, D. Johann Sebastian Bach. 1960.
14. Jemnitz, S.   Fryderyk Chopin. 1960.
15. Bónis, F. Mosonyi Mihály. 1960.
16. Szőllősy, A. Arthur Honegger. 1960.
17. Kroó, G. Hector Berlioz. 1960.
18. Balogh, P.A. Jean Sibelius. 1961.
19. Pándi, M. Claudio Monteverdi. 1961.
20. Eősze, L. Giuseppe Verdi. 1961?.
21. Jemnitz, S. Wolfgang Amadeus Mozart. 1961.
22. Fajth, T. Gioacchino Rossini. 1962.

Klasikové hudební vědy a kritiky [Ř. 1, Sv. 1: Klasikové
    české hudební. . .]. Řídí Ivan Vojtěch.
Praha: SNKLHU, later SHV

Řada 1
1. Helfert, V. Tvůrčí rozvoj Bedřicha Smetany; preludium k životnímu dílu. 2. vyd. 1953.
1. ----. Smetanovské kapitoly. 1954.
2. ----. O české hudbě. 1957.
3. Procházka, L. Slavná doba české hudby; výbor z kritik a článků. 1958.
4. Hostinský, O. O hudbě. Sest. Miloslav Nedbal. 1961.
Řada 2
1. Liszt o svých současnících. Přel. Z. Lacinová. 1956.
2. Wagner, R. O hudbě a o umění. Výběr statí z originálu Gesammelte Schriften und Dichtungen. Přel. Jitka Fučíková a Hana Šnajdrová. 1959.
3. Schumann - o hudbě a hudebnících. Přel. F. Wünschová. 1960.
4. Stasov, V. Vasil'evich. O ruské hudební klasice. 1960.

Kleine Bücherei des Harmonika-Freundes. Hrsg. von Armin Fett.
Trossingen/Württemberg: M. Hohner
1. Fett, A., & E. Pelz. Harmonika-Tabellen; Wissenswertes über Harmonika-Instrumente. 1952. 5. verbesserte Aufl., mit Anhang "Elektronische Instrumente." 1964.
2. Fett, A. Kleine Musiklehre. 1952.
3. ----. Der Aufbau einer musikalischen Vortragsfolge; Ratschläge zur Programmgestaltung. 1952.
4. Feil, E. Die Mundharmonika; kleine Instrumentenkunde. 1955.
5. Fett, A. Was der Leiter einer Handharmonika-Spielgruppe wissen muss. 1. Teil: Instrumenten- und Partiturkunde. 195-.
6. Bilger, Walter. Wie gründe und leite ich ein Handharmonika-Orchestra? 1953.
7. Karow, H. Die Vorbereitung eines Harmonika-

Konzertes. 1953.

8. Fett, A. Kleine Harmonielehre. 1953.
9. Friedrich, W. Gebundene Improvisation. 1958.
10. Messner, W. Kleine Reparaturkunde. 195- .
11. Fett, A. Kleine Dirigierlehre. 1. Teil. 2. Aufl. 1958.
12. ----. Die Register und ihre Anwendung. 1955.
13. ----. Was der Leiter einer Harmonika-Spielgruppe wissen muss. Teil 2. 1956.
14. ----. Das Akkordeon; kleine Instrumentenkunde. 1956.
15. ----. Die Handharmonika; Wiener Instrumente und Club-Modelle. Kleine Instrumentenkunde. 1956.
16. ----. Kleine Dirigierlehre. 2. Teil. In prep.

Kleine Jazz-Bibliothek. Hrsg. von J. Slawe (pseud. for Jan Sypniewski).
Basel: Verlag National-Zeitung (No. 1): Papillons-Verlag (No. 2)

1. Slawe, J., pseud. Einführung in die Jazzmusik. 1948.
2. ----. Louis Armstrong; zehn monographische Studien. 1953.

Das kleine Musikbuch
Reutlingen: Edition Tonos

1. Goethe, J. W. von. Mit Goethe ins Konzert. Worte des Dichters zu Chören und Liedern. Verfasser: H. Günther, A. Aldefeld, P. Seifert. 1949.

Kleine Musikbücherei
Hamburg: H. Sikorski

1. Steffin, J. F.   Johann Sebastian Bach; Leben und Werk. 1953.
2. Fellerer, K. G. Georg Friedrich Händel; Leben und Werk. 1953.
3. Farga, F. Christoph Willibald Gluck; Leben und Werk. 1953.
4. Baresel, A. Joseph Haydn; Leben und Werk. 1953.

5. Baresel, A. Wolfgang Amadeus Mozart; Leben und Werk. 1956.
6. Marein, J. Ludwig van Beethoven. Did not appear?
7. Steffin, J. F. Franz Schubert; Leben und Werk. 1954.
8. Baresel, A. Giacomo Puccini; Leben und Werk. 1954.
9. Fellerer, K. G. Anton Bruckner. Did not appear?
10. Baresel, A. Richard Strauss; Leben und Werk. 1953.
11. Moser, H. J. Blinde Musiker aus sieben Jahrhunderten. 1956.
12. Jacob, W. P. Richard Wagner; Leben und Werk. 1958.
Unnumbered
   Nick, E. Paul Lincke. 1953.
   ----. Vom Wiener Walzer zur Wiener Operette. 1954.

Knihovna klasiků. Musikologické spisy.
Praha: SNKL
6. Rolland, R. Händel. 1959.
7. ----. Beethoven III. 1959.

Knižníce hudebních rozhledů
Praha: SCS, later Panton
Roč. 1
1. Za rozkvět nové zábavné hudby. 1955. Contributions by
   Jan F. Fischer, Theodor Hirner, Josef Brachtl, &
   Jan Seidl.
4. Sádecký, Z. O některých otázkách estetiky O. Hostinské-
   ho; studie. 1955.
Roč. 2
3. Jiránek, J. Vít Nejedlý; kritiky a stati o hudbě
   (1934-1944). 1956.
5. Stanislav, J. Zo vzťahov medzi rečou, hudbou a spevom.
   Also: Kresánek, J. K problematike uměleckého majstrov-
   stva. 1956.
6. Barvík, M. Milan Harašta (1919-1946); nedokončený
   život a dílo skladatele. 1956.
7. Smetana, R. O místo a význam Dvořákova skladatelského

97

díla v českém hudebním vývoji. 1956.

8. Válek, J. Písně radosti a mládí; umělecký vývoj a dílo Radima Drejsla. 1956.

9. Dokumenty boje o hudební výchovu; materiály z Celostátní konference Svazu čs. skladatelů o hudební výchově lidu v Praze 28. dubna 1956. 1956.

Roč. 2, mimořadný sv. Szabolcsi, B. Život Bély Bartôka. Z mad'arštiny přel. Mila Zadražilová. Úvod napsal Fr. A. Kypta. 1956.

Roč. 3

1. Zich, J. Instrumentační práce se skupinami. 1957.

2. Risinger, K. Nástin obecného hudebního funkčního systému rozšířene tonality. 1957.

3/4. Paclt, J. Tři kapitoly o Zdeňku Nejedlêm; zrození vědce, mistr kritiky, estetika hudební kritiky. 1957.

5. Pilka, J. Filmová hudba Jiřího Srnky. 1957.

6/7. Stanislav, J. Stati a kritiky. Sestavil Jiří Macek. 1957.

Roč. 4

1. Stará, V., ed. Ervín Schulhoff, Vzpomínky, studie e dokumenty. 1958.

2. Rektorys, A. Naši operní pěvci. 1958.

3. Janeček, K. Vyjádření souzvuků; kapitola ze "Základů temperované harmonie." 1958.

6/7. Jiránek, J. Jaroslav Teklý; sborník vzpomínek, hudebních kritik a písní. 1958.

Roč. 5

1. Pensdorfová, E. Klasický základ české hry se zpěvy a tanci; k problematice hudby k Tylovu "Strakonickému dudákovi." 1959.

2. Havlíček, D. O novou českou taneční hudbu; vývojové tendence taneční hudby v ČSR v letech 1945-1958. 1959.

3/4. Mařík, J. M. Anglická hudba. 1959.

5/6. Leoš Janáček; sborník statí a studif. 1959.

7/8. Gregor, V. Česká dětská píseň umělá; piseň jednohlasá s průvodem klavíru, houslí nebo orchestru. 1959.

9. Štědroň, B. Dílo Leoše Janáčka; abecední seznam Janáčkových skladeb a úprav, bibliografie a diskografie. Sest. a úvodní profil napsal B.S. 1959.

11/13. Druhý sjezd Svazu československých skladatelů v Praze ve dnech 25.-28. února 1959; materiály a dokumenty. 1959.

Řada A

1. Vratislavský, J. Moravské kvarteto, 1923-1955. 1961.

2/3. Volek, J. Novodobé harmonické systémy z hlediska vědecké filosofie. 1961.

4. Pospíšil, V. Václav Talich; několik kapitol o díle a životě českého umělce. 1961.

6. Stanislav, J. Ludvík Kuba; zakladatel slovenské hudební folkoristiky. 1963.

Řada B: Hudební věda; studie Kabinetu pro soudobou hudbu.

Sborník. Řídí Jaroslav Jiránek a Bohumil Karásek. 1962- . Yearbook; outside the scope of this study. The contents for 1961 (Nos. 1-4) and 1962 (Nos. 1-2) are listed on pp. 397-98 of 1962 (Nos. 3/4).

Kölner Beiträge zur Musikforschung. Hrsg. von Karl Gustav Fellerer.

Regensburg: G. Bosse

1. Kahl, W. Verzeichnis des Schrifttums über Franz Schubert. 1938.

2. Gröninger, E. Repertoire-Untersuchungen zum mehrstimmigen Notre Dame Conductus. 1939.

3. Reimann, M. Untersuchungen zur Formgeschichte der französischen Klavier-Suite, mit besonderer Berücksichtigung von Couperins "Ordres." 1940.

4. Martin, B. Untersuchungen zur Struktur der "Kunst der Fuge" J.S. Bach. 1941.

5. Fellerer, K.G. Deutsche Gregorianik in Frankreich. 1942.

6. Schneider, M. Die Orgelspieltechnik des frühen 19. Jahrhunderts in Deutschland, dargestellt an den Orgelschulen der Zeit. 1943.

7. Ewerhart, R. Die Handschrift 322/1994 der Stadtbibliothek Trier als musikalische Quelle. 1955.

8. Wehmeyer, G. Max Reger als Liederkomponist; ein Beitrag zum Problem der Wort-Ton-Beziehung. 1955.

9. Aengenvoort, J. Quellen und Studien zur Geschichte des Graduale Monasteriense. 1955.

10. Kirchmeyer, H. Igor Strawinsky; Zeitgeschichte im Persönlichkeitsbild. 1958.

11. Unger, U. Die Klavierfuge im zwanzigsten Jahrhundert. 2. unveränderte Auflage 1956.

12. Busch, G. C. Ph. E. Bach und seine Lieder. 1957.

13. Blindow, M. Die Choralbegleitung des 18. Jahrhunderts in der evangelischen Kirche Deutschlands. 1957.

14. Roth, J. Die mehrstimmigen lateinischen Litaneikompositionen des 16. Jahrhunderts. 1959.

15. Göller, G. Vinzenz von Beauvais, O. P. [um 1194-1264] und sein Musiktraktat im Speculum doctrinale 1959.

16. Fricke, J. Ueber subjektive Differenztöne höchster hörbarer Töne und des angrenzenden Ultraschalls im musikalischen Hören. 1960.

17. Onkelbach, F. Lucas Lossius und seine Musiklehre. 1960.

18. Friedrich, A. Beiträge zur Geschichte des weltlichen Frauenchores im 19. Jahrhundert in Deutschland. 1961.

19. Khatschi Khatschi. Dhastgah; Studien zur neuen persischen Musik. 1962.

20. Hüschen, H. Untersuchungen zu den Textkonkordanzen im Musikschrifttum des Mittelalters.

21. Bäcker, U. Frankreichs Moderne von Claude Debussy bis Pierre Boulez. 1962.

22. Rouvel, D. Zur Geschichte der Musik am Fürstlich Waldeckschen Hofe zu Arolsen. 1962.

23. Kuckertz, J. Gestaltvariation in den von Bartók gesam-

melten rumänischen Colinden. I: Text. II: Notenteil.
1963.
24. Schulte-Bunert, D. Die deutsche Klaviersonate des 20.
Jahrhunderts; eine Formuntersuchung der deutschen
Klaviersonaten der Zwanziger Jahre. 1963.
25. Rothärmel, M. Der musikalische Zeitbegriff seit
Moritz Hauptmann. 1963.
26. Müller-Heuser, F. Vox humana; ein Beitrag zur Untersuchung der Stimmästhetik des Mittelalters. 1963.
28. Härting, M. Der Messgesang im Braunschweiger
Domstift St. Blasii. 1964?

Kontrapunkte; Schriften zur Deutschen Musik der Gegenwart.
Hrsg. von Heinrich Lindlar.
Rodenkirchen: P. J. Tonger
 1. Mersmann, H. Deutsche Musik des XX. Jahrhunderts
im Spiegel des Weltgeschehens. 1958.
 2. Die Stimme der Komponisten; 24 Reden, Briefe, Aufsätze aus den Jahren 1907-1958. 1959.
 3. Erpf, H. Wie soll es weitergehen? 1958.
 4. Lindlar, H., ed. Wolfgang Fortner; eine Monographie.
1960.
 5. Kolneder, W. Anton Webern; Einführung in Werk und
Stil. 1961.
 6. Wörner, K.H. Karlheinz Stockhausen; Werk, Wollen
1950-1962. 1963.
 7. Mersmann, H. Lebensraum der Musik; Aufsätze,
Ansprachen. 1964.
 8. Reich, W. Alban Berg; Umwelt und Persönlichkeitsbild.
In prep.
 9. Lindlar, H. Im Zwielicht der Zeit; Musik-Kritiken, Kommentare, 1950-1962. In prep.

Künstler der Schallplatte
Bielefeld: Bielefelder Verlagsanstalt
 1. Voss, C.D. Bildband für Schlagerfreunde. 1961.

2. Voss, C. D. Bildband für Freunde von Oper und Konzert. 1961.

Kurze Biographien grosser Komponisten
Tokyo: Daisan Shobô
1. Netke, M. Ludwig van Beethoven. 1957.
2. ----. Wolfgang Amadeus Mozart. Erl. von H. Gokita. 1958.
3. ----. Johann Sebastian Bach. Erl. von Y. Sugiyama. 1958.
4. ----. Robert Schumann. Erl. von O. Ueno. 1959.
5. ----. Franz Schubert. Erl. von H. Gokita. 1959.

Kustannustalon musiikkiopas
Helsingissä: Kustannustalo
1. Ringbom, N.-E.   Säveltaide. Suomentanut Tauno Pylkkänen. 1946.
2. Gray, C. Sibeliuksen sinfoniat. Suomentanut sekä huomautuksilla ja lisäyksillä varustanut Jussi Jalas. 1945.

Leren luisteren. Onder de leiding van Dr. M. Boereboom.
Antwerpen: De Nederlandsche Boekhandel
1. Boereboom, M. Symfonie nr 4 in E klein, op. 98, van Johannes Brahms. 1962.
2. Ackere, J. van. Images voor orkest van Claude Debussy. 1962.
3. Corbet, A. Carmen; opera in 4 bedrijven van H. Meilhac en L. Halévy naar de novelle van Prosper Mérimêe. Muziek van Georges Bizet. 1962.
4. Broeckx, J. L. De liedkunst van Hugo Wolf. 1962.
5. Van der Mueren, F. De zee; simfonisch gedicht. Muziek van Paul Gilson. 1962.

Literarhistorisch-musikwissenschaftliche Abhandlungen. Hrsg. von Friedrich Gennrich.
Würzburg: K. Triltsch
1. Kuhlmann, G. Die zweistimmigen französischen Motetten des Kodex Montpellier, Faculté de Médecine H. 196, in

ihrer Bedeutung für die Musikgeschichte des 13. Jahrhunderts. 1938.

2. ----. Uebertragungen der zweistimmigen französischen Motetten von Mo 6 und Kommentare. 1938.

3. Schulz, H. -G. Musikalischer Impressionismus und impressionistischer Klavierstil; ein Beitrag zur musikalischen Stilforschung. 1938.

4. Kern, H. Franz Vollrath Buttstett (1735-1814); eine Studie zur Musik des Spätbarock. 1939.

5. Friedwagner, M. Rumänische Volkslieder aus der Bukowina. 1. Band: Liebeslieder. 1940.

6. Sorgatz, H. Musiker und Musikanten als dichterisches Motiv; eine Studie zur Auffassung und Gestaltung des Musikers in der erzählenden Dichtung von Sturm und Drang bis zum Realismus. 1939.

7. Kosel, A. Sebald Heyden (1499-1561); ein Beitrag zur Geschichte der Nürnberger Schulmusik in der Reformationszeit. 1940.

8. Erhlinger, F. Georg Friedrich Händels Orgelkonzerte. 1941.

9. Zitzmann, R. Die Melodien der Kolmarer Liederhandschrift in ihrer Bedeutung für die Musik- und Stilgeschichte der Gotik. 1944.

10. Engelmann, H. U. Béla Bartóks Mikrokosmos; Versuch einer Typologie "Neuer Musik. " 1953.

11. Bittinger, W. Studien zur musikalischen Textkritik des mittelalterlichen Liedes. 1953.

12. Hamm, W. Studien über Ernst Peppings drei Klaviersonaten 1937. 1955.

13. Krieg, E. Das lateinische Osterspiel von Tours; aus der Handschrift 927 der Stadtbibliothek. 1956.

14. Forneberg, E. W. A. Mozart; Lebens- und Werkstil, synaesthetisch-typologischer Vergleich mit Bach-Beethoven und Goethe-Schiller. 1956.

15. ----. Der Geist der neuen Musik; der neue Klang im Spiegel der traditionellen Harmonielehre. 1957.

16. Jakobik, A. Zur Einheit der neuen Musik. 1957.

17. Schilling, H. L. Paul Hindemiths "Cardillac"; Beiträge zu einem Vergleich der beiden Opernfassungen--Stil-

kriterien im Schaffen Hindemiths. 1962.

Magyar zenetudomány. Szerkeszti Bónis Ferenc.
Budapest: Zeneműkiadó Vállalat
1. Szabolcsi, B. A magyar zene évszázadai. Tanulmányok.
   1: A középkortól a XVII. századig. 1959.
2. ----. A magyar zene évszázadai. Tanulmányok. 2:
   XVIII-XIX. század. 1961.
3. Molnár, A. Irások a zenéről; válogatott cikkek és tanulmányok. 1961.
4. Legány, D. A magyar zene krónikája; zenei művelődésünk ezer éve dokumentumokban. 1962.

Les Maîtres du jazz
Paris: Éd. du Belvédère
1. Panassié, H. Louis Armstrong. 1949.

Mała biblioteka operowa. Redaktor cyklu: Mieczysław Tomaszewski.
Kraków: PWM
1. Rudziński, W. Co to jest opera. Wyd. 2. 1960.
2. Poźniak, W. Wesele Figara W.A. Mozarta. 1956.
3. ----. Cyrulik Sewilski J. Rossiniego. 1955?
4. Rudziński, W. Halka S. Moniuszki. 1954.
5. Gołowiński, G. Kniaź Igor A. Borodina. 1955.
6. Prószyński, S. Tosca J. Pucciniego. 1956.
7. Rudziński, W. Straszny Dwór S. Moniuszki. 1956
8. Stromenger, K. Uprowadzenie z seraju W.A. Mozarta.
   1957.
9. Swolkień, H. Traviata J. Verdiego. 1957.
10. Stromenger, K. Złoty Kogucik M. Rimskiego-Korsakowa.
    1956.
11. Swolkień, H. Rigoletto J. Verdiego. 1958.
12. Lissa, Z. Bunt żaków T. Szeligowskiego. 1955. Wyd.
    2. 1957.
13. Prószyński, S. Aida J. Verdiego. 1958.

14. Młodziejowski, J. Sprzedana Narzeczona Fryderyka
Smetany. 1958.
15. Swolkień, H. Otello J. Verdiego. 1960.
16. Prószyński, S. Cyganeria J. Pucciniego. 1961.
17. Gabryś, J. Carmen J. Bizeta. 1961.

Małe monografie muzyczne. Redaktor cyklu: Stefania
Łobaczewska.
Kraków: PWM
1. Łobaczewska, S. Ludwik van Beethoven. 1953. Wyd. 2.
1955.
2. Marek, T. Schubert. 1952. Wyd. 2., uzup. 1955.
3. Jarociński, S. Wolfgang Amadeusz Mozart. 1954.
Wyd. 2., uzup. 1956.
4. Rudziński, W. Moniuszko. 1954. Wyd. 2., uzup. 1957.
5. Strumiłło, T. Szkice z polskiego życia muzycznego XIX
wieku. 1954.
6. Iwaszkiewicz, J. Chopin. 1955. Wyd. 2. 1956.
7. Sołowcow, A. Rimsky-Korsakov. Tłum. M. Zagórska.
1956.
8. Rolland, R. Haendel. Tłum. M. Jarocińska. 1958.
9. Powroźniak, J. Paganini. 1958.
In preperation
Lissa, Z. Czajkowski.
Marek, T. Haydn.
Jarociński, S. Debussy.
Šourek, O. Dworzak.

Man and His Music
Fair Lawn, N. J. : Essential Books
1. Harman, A. Mediaeval and Early Renaissance Music
(up to c. 1525). 1958.
2. Harman, A., & A. Milner. Late Renaissance and
Baroque Music (c. 1525-c. 1750). 1959.
3. Mellers, W. H. The Sonata Principle (from c. 1750).
1957.

4. ----. Romanticism and the 20th Century (from 1800). 1957.

Vols. 1-4 issued in one volume: Alex Harman & Wilfrid Mellers, Man and His Music; The Story of Musical Experience in the West (London: Oxford Univ. Press, 1962).

Materiały do bibliografii muzyki polskiej. Redaktor serii Tadeusz Strumiłło (1-3).
Kraków: PWM
1. Michałowski, K. Opery polskie. 1954.
2. Nowaczyk, E. Pieśni solowe Stanisława Moniuszki; katalog tematyczny. 1954.
3. Michałowski, K. Bibliografia polskiego piśmiennictwa muzycznego. 1955.
4. ----. Bibliografia polskiego piśmiennictwa muzycznego. Suplement 1955-1963. 1964.

Meister der leichten Musik
Zürich: Amalthea-Verlag
1. Appeared under the title Meister der Operette.
2. Ewen, D. George Gershwin; Leben und Werk. Ueber-tragung und Bearbeitung von G. Martin. 1955.

Meister der Operette
Zürich: Amalthea-Verlag
1. Oesterreicher, R. Emmerich Kálmán; der Weg eines Komponisten. 1954.

Merlin Music Books
New York: Merlin Press. Partly numbered.
1. Schrade, L. Bach; The Conflict Between the Sacred and the Secular. 1955.
2. Stevens, D. Tudor Church Music. 1955.
3. Strobel, H. Stravinsky; Classic Humanist. Trans. from the German by Hans Rosenwald. 1955.

4. Lesure, F. Musicians and Poets of the French Renaissance. Trans. from the French by Elio Gianturco and Hans Rosenwald. 1955.
5. Georgiades, T. Greek Music, Verse, and Dance. Trans. from the German by Edwin Benedikt and Marie Louise Martinez. 1956.
6. Sessions, R. Reflections on the Music Life in the United States. 1956.
7. Ronga, L. The Meeting of Poetry and Music. Trans. from the Italian by Elio Gianturco and Cara Rosanti. 1956.
8. Rostand, C. French Music Today. Translated from the French by Henry Marx. 1957.
No others appeared.

Methodische Beiträge zum Unterricht im Fach Musik. Hrsg. vom Deutschen Pädagogischen Zentralinstitut, Sektion Unterrichtsmethodik und Lehrpläne.
Berlin: Volk und Wissen Volkseigener Verlag
1. Bimberg, S. Feiergestaltung in der Schule. 1962.
2. Erläuterungen zum Musikunterricht in der 5. Klasse. Ausgearbeitet von einer Arbeitsgruppe von Musikerziehern unter Leitung von Erdmann Bogisch. 1963.

Mitteilungen der Kommission für Musikforschung. Sonderabdrucke aus dem Anzeiger der phil. -hist. Klasse der Oesterreichischen Akademie der Wissenschaften.
Wien: Rohrer in Kommission, später Böhlau in Kommission
1. Wessely, O. Zur Frage nach der Herkunft Arnolds von Bruck. 1955.
2. ----. Neues zur Lebensgeschichte von Erasmus Lapicida. 1955.
3. ----. Neue Hofhaimeriana. 1955.
4. Nemeth, C. Zur Lebensgeschichte von Carlo Agostino Badia (1672-1738). 1955.
5. Wessely, O. Beiträge zur Geschichte der maximiliani-

schen Hofkapelle. 1956.

6. Federhofer, H. Die Niederländer an den Habsburger-höfen in Oesterreich. 1956.

7. Schenk, E. Zwei unbekannte Frühwerke von Franz Schmidt. 1956.

8. Nettl, P. Das Prager Quartierbuch des Personals der Krönungsoper 1723. 1957.

9. Kellner, A. Ein Mensuraltraktat aus der Zeit um 1400. 1957.

10. Wessely, O. Zu Leben und Werk von Matthäus Gugl. 1957.

11. Osthoff, W. Zur Bologneser Aufführung von Monteverdis "Ritorno di Ulisse" im Jahre 1640. 1958.

12. Wessely, O. Ein unbekanntes Huldigungsgedicht auf Heinrich Schütz. 1961.

13. Schaal, R. Quellen zu Johann Kaspar Kerll. 1962.

14. Schenk, E. Ein unbekanntes Klavier-Uebungsstück Mozarts. 1962.

Monografías del Centro de Estudios Folclóricos y Musicales, Bogotá.

Bogotá: Centro de Estudios Folclóricos y Musicales

1. Pardo Tovar, A. Los cantares tradicionales del Baudó. 1960.

2. Pardo Tovar, A., & J. Pinzón Urrea. Rítmica y melódica del folclor chocoano. 1961.

3. Pardo Tovar, A., & J. Bermúdez Silva. La guitarrería popular de Chiquinquirá. Apendice; Fotografías documentales. 1963.

4. Stevenson, R. La música colonial en Colombia. In prep.

5. Pardo Tovar, A. Del folclor en Colombia. In prep.

6. Pardo Tovar, A., & B. Emilio Atehortúa. Anotaciones sobre el cancionero ritual del Chocó. In prep.

Monographs in Theory and Composition

108

Baldwin, N. Y.: Music Teachers National Association
1. Forte, A. The Compositional Matrix. 1961.

Monographs on the Art of Piano Teaching
London: Walsh, Holmes
1. Reeves, B., pseud. Ourselves and Our Pupils; A
   Discussion On the Human Factor in Teaching. 1951.
2. ----. Aural Training. 1951.

Moravian Music Foundation Publications
Winston-Salem, N. Car.: Moravian Music Foundation
1. McCorkle, D. M. The Moravian Contribution to American Music. 1956. Reprinted from MLA Notes, Sept.,
   1956.
2. ----. John Antes, "American Dilettante." 1956. Reprinted from The Musical Quarterly, Oct., 1956.
3. ----. The Collegium Musicum Salem; Its Music, Musicians and Importance. 1956. Reprinted from the North
   Carolina Historical Review, Oct., 1956.
4. Grider, R. A. Historical Notes on Music in Bethlehem,
   Pa. (From 1741-1871). With a Foreword by Donald M.
   McCorkle. 1957. Reprinted from the original ed. of
   1873.
5. Leinbach, J. Regiment Band of the Twenty-Sixth North
   Carolina. Edited by Donald M. McCorkle. 1958.
   Reprinted from Civil War History, Sept., 1958.
6. David, H. T. Musical Life in the Pennsylvania Settle-
   ments of the Unitas Fratrum. With a Foreword by
   Donald M. McCorkle. 1959. Reprinted from Transactions
   of the Moravian Historical Society, 1942.

Münchner Veröffentlichungen zur Musikgeschichte. Hrsg.
   von Thrasybulos G. Georgiades.
Tutzing: Hans Schneider
1. Herrmann-Bengen, I. Tempobezeichnungen; Ursprung,
   Wandel im 17. und 18. Jahrhundert. 1959.

2. Zaminer, F. Der vatikanische Organum-Traktat (Ottob. lat. 3025); Organum-Praxis der frühen Notre Dame-Schule und ihrer Vorstufen. 1959.
3. Osthoff, W. Monteverdistudien. 1. Bd.: Das dramatische Spätwerk Claudio Monteverdis. 1960.
4. Hermelink, S. Dispositiones modorum; die Tonarten in der Musik Palestrinas und seiner Zeitgenossen. 1960.
5. Bockholdt, R. Die frühen Messenkompositionen von Guillaume Dufay. 1960.
6. Göllner, T. Formen früher Mehrstimmigkeit in deutschen Handschriften des späten Mittelalters. Mit Veröffentlichung der Orgelspiellehre aus dem. Cod. lat. 7755 der Bayerischen Staatsbibliothek München. 1961.
7. Eppelsheim, J. Das Orchester in den Werken Jean-Baptiste Lullys. 1961.
8. Kunze, S. Die Instrumentalmusik Giovanni Gabrielis. Mit einem Notenanhang. 1963.
9. Martinez, M. L. Die Musik des frühen Trecento. 1963.

Museo Histórico Nacional. Sección de Musicología.
Montevideo, Uruguay; Museo Histórico Nacional, Sección de Musicología.
1. Ayestarán, L. Luis Sambucetti; vida y obra. 1956.
2. ----. Domenico Zipoli; vida y obra. 1962.
3. ----. Bibliografía de la música en el Uruguay. 1: Libros e revistas. 2: Música. In prep.

Music From the Belfry
Sellersville, Penna.: Schulmerich Electronics
1. Bigelow, A. L. English Type Carillonic Bells; Their History and Music. 1949.
No more published.

Music Library Manuals
Berkeley, Calif.: University of California Library. Only Nos. 3 & 4 appeared.

3. The General Library, University of California. Manual for the Phonorecord Cataloger. Prepared by Merle C. Bartlett. 1953.
4. ----. Duties of the Clerk Assigned to Phonorecord Cataloger. Prepared by Merle C. Bartlett. 1953.

Music Theory Translation Series. Ed. by Richard L. Crocker.
New Haven, Conn.: Yale School of Music
1. Gasparini, F. The Practical Harmonist at the Harpsichord. Trans. by Frank S. Stillings; ed. by David L. Burrows. 1963.

Música en Compostela
Madrid: Dirección General de Relaciones Culturales
2. Jacobs, C. La interpretación de la música española del siglo XVI para instrumentos de teclado. 1959.

La Musica moderna
Milano: Il Balcone
1. Mila, M.   Saggi mozartiani. 1945.
2. Malipiero, G. F. Cossi' va lo mondo. 1945?
3. Gavazzeni, G. Parole e suoni. 1946.
4. Mantelli, A. Tre secoli di musica europea; musica strumentale dal '500 al '700. 1946.
   Gui, V. Il tempo che fu.
   Paoli, R. Coro unanime.

Musical Theorists in Translation
Brooklyn: Institute of Mediaeval Music
1. Anonymous IV. Concerning the Measurement of Polyphonic Song. Trans. and ed. by Luther Dittmer. 1959.
2. Robert de Handlo. The Rules with Maxims of Master Franco. Trans. and ed. by Luther Dittmer. 1959.
3. Nivers, G. G. Treatise on the Composition of Music. Trans. and ed. by Albert Cohen. 1961.

4. Huygens. Use and Nonuse of the Organ.
5. Bernier. Treatise on Composition.

Musica-serie; kleine boeken over grote mannen
Den Haag: J. P. Kruseman
1. Vos, A. C. Het leven van Franz Liszt. 1949?
2. Prick van Wely, M. A. Het leven van Frêdêric Chopin.
   1949?
3. ----. Het leven van Wolfgang Amadeus Mozart. 1949?
4. Vos, A. C. Het leven van Ludwig van Beethoven. 1949?
5. Prick van Wely, M. A. Het leven van Richard Wagner.
   1950.
6. Vos, A. C. Het leven van Peter Iljitsj Tsjaikofsky. 1950.
7. Verhaar, A. Het leven van Franz Schubert. 1950.
8. Vos, A. C. Het leven van Johann Sebastian Bach. 1950.
9. Verhaar, A. Het leven van Claude Debussy. 195-.
10. Vos, A. C. Het leven van Robert Schumann. 195-.
11. Prick van Wely, M. A. Het leven van Louis Hector
    Berlioz. 195-.
12. Vos, A. C. Het leven van Felix Mendelssohn-Bartholdy.
    195-.
13. ----. Het leven van Maurice Ravel. 195-.
14. Verhaar, A. Het leven van Bêla Bartôk. 1951?
15. Vos, A. C. Het leven van Joseph Haydn. 195-.
16. ----. Het leven van Edvard Grieg. 1951?
17. ----. Het leven van Georg Friedrich Händel. 195-.
18. Backers, C. Het leven van Giacomo Puccini. 195-.
19. ----. Het leven van George Gershwin. 195-.

Musices graecai corrigenda
Paris: M. Dabo-Peranić
1. Dabo-Peranić, M.   Les harmonies grecques clas-
   siques, ces inconnues. Prêface de M. Armand Machabey.
   1959.
No others published.

112

Musiche e musicisti pugliesi
Bari: Società di Storia Patria per la Puglia
1. Casavola, F. Tommaso Traetta di Bitonto (1727-1779); la vita e le opere. Con un premessa di Pier Fausto Palumbo. 1957.

Musiciens de tous les temps
Paris: Éditions Seghers
1. Hofmann, R. Dimitri Chostakovitch; l'homme et son oeuvre. 1963.
2. ----. Serge Prokofiev; l'homme et son oeuvre. 1964.
3. Vignal, M. Franz-Joseph Haydn; l'homme et son oeuvre. 1964.

Musiciens et leurs oeuvres. Collection dirigée par Alfred Pochon.
Lausanne: F. Rouge
1. Buenzod, E. Musiciens. 1945. Contents: Bach, Beethoven, Haydn, Mendelssohn, Schumann, Berlioz, Brahms, Franck, Moussorgski, Debussy.
6. ----. Musiciens; 2. sér. 1949. Contents: Haendel, Mozart, Schubert, Weber, Rossini, Liszt, Wagner, Bizet, Ravel, Strawinsky.

Musicisti della nostra terra. Diretta da Renzo Martini.
Magenta: A. Drago
1. Martini, R. Ildebrando Pizzetti.
2. ----. Arturo Toscanini.
3. ----. Vita di un musicista permense [Arnaldo Furlotti]. 1949.
4. ----. Costantino Dall'Argine.
5. ----. Cleofonte Campanini.
6. ----. Ferdinando Paër.
We have not verified the appearance of vols. 1-2, 4-6.

Musicisti italiani dell'800

Milano: Editrice Athena
1. Toni, A. Antonio Bazzini. 1946.
2. ----. Vittorio Maria Vanzo. 1946.

Musicologica. In Verbindung mit J. Chailley, E. Reeser,
A. van der Linden, J. Kunst, hrsg. von H. Husmann.
Leiden: E. J. Brill
1. Raynaud, G. Bibliographie des altfranzösischen Liedes.
Neu bearbeitet und ergänzt von H. Spanke. Teil 1.
1955.

Musicologica medii aevi. Ed. by Joseph Smits van Waes-
berghe.
Amsterdam: Noord-Hollandsche Uitgevers Maatschappij
1. Smits van Waesberghe, J., ed. Espositiones in Mi-
crologum Guidonis Aretini. Liber Argumentorum, Liber
Specierum, Metrologus, Commentarius in Micrologum
Guidonis Aretini. 1957.
2. ----. De melodieën van Hendrik van Veldekes liederen.
Rede uitgesproken aan de Universiteit van Amsterdam op
Maandag, 4 November 1957. 1957.

Musicological Studies; Wissenschaftliche Abhandlungen
Brooklyn: Institute of Mediaeval Music
1. Dittmer, L. Auszug aus The Worcester Music Fragments. 1958.
2. Schuetze, G. C., Jr. An Introduction to Faugues. 1960.
3. Trumble, E. Fauxbourdon; an Historical Survey. Vol.
1. 1959.
4. Spiess, L. B. Historical Musicology. With articles by
E. Krohn, L. Hibberd, L. Dittmer, Tsang-Houei, T.
Minagawa, and Z. Nováček. 1963.
5. Levarie, S. Fundamentals of Harmony. 1962.
6. Southern, E. The Buxheim Organ Book. 1963.
7. Dittmer, L. Repertorium organorum (F. Ludwig).
Vol. 1. Part 1.

Musicological Studies and Documents. Armen Carapetyan, General Editor.

Rome or elsewhere: American Institute of Musicology
1. Smits van Waesberghe, J. Cymbala. 1951.
2. Dittmer, L. A. The Worcester Fragments; A Catalogue Raisonné and Transcription. With a Foreword by Dom Anselm Hughes, O. S. B. 1957.
3. Mei, G. Letters on Ancient and Modern Music to Vincenzo Galilei and Giovanni Bardi; A Study with Annotated Texts by Claude V. Palisca. 1960.
4. Muffat, G. An Essay on Thoroughbass. Ed. with an Intro. by Hellmut Federhofer. 1961.
5. Tinctoris, J. The Art of Counterpoint; "Liber de arte Contrapuncti." Trans. and ed. with an Intro. by Albert Seay. 1961.
6. Glareanus, H. Dodecachordon. Trans. and ed. by Clement A. Miller.
7. Stäblein-Harder, H. Fourteenth-Century Mass Music in France; Critical Text. Companion Volume to Corpus Mensurabilis Musicae, 29. 1962.
8. Descartes, R. Compendium of Music. Trans. by Walter Robert, Intro. and notes by Charles Kent. 1961.
9. Bottrigari, H. Il Desiderio; Or, Concerning the Playing Together of Various Musical Instruments.
Also: Vicenzo Giustiniani. Discorso sopra la musica.
Trans. by Carol MacClintock. 1962.
10. Codex Faenza, Bibl. Comunale, 117. A facsimile edition presented by Armen Carapetyan. 1961.
11. Vicentino, N. Life and Works, by Henry W. Kaufmann. 1964.
12. Compère, L. Life and Works, by Ludwig Finscher. 1964.
13. Ms London British Museum Add. 29987. A facsimile with an Introduction by Gilbert Reaney.
14. Haar, J. The Tugendsterne of Harsdöffer & Staden; An Exercise in Musical Humanism. 1964.

15. Maillard, J. Lais & Chansons d'Ernoul de Gastinois. 1964.
16. Kenton, E. The Life and Works of Giovanni Gabrieli. In prep.
17. MacClintock, C. The Life and Works of Giaches Wert. In prep.
18. Warren, E. B. The Life and Works of Robert Fayrfax. In prep.
19. Allaire, G. The Problem of Accidentals in Polyphony. In prep.
20. Hoppin, R. H. The Cypriot Manuscript, Turin, National Library, J. H. 9. In prep.

Musiekbiblioteek
Kaapstad: Tafelberg
1. Du Plessis, H. Johann Sebastian Bach; 'n biografie en ag opstelle. 1960.

Musik aus der Steiermark. Reihe 4: Beiträge zur steirischen Musikforschung.
Graz: Akademische Druck- und Verlagsanstalt
2. Suppan, W. Heinrich Eduard Josef von Lannoy (1787-1853); Leben und Werke. 1960.
3. ----. Hanns Holenia. 1960.
4. Rappold, K. Die Entwicklung des Männerchorwesens in der Steiermark. 1963.

Musik der Zeit; eine Schriftenreihe zur zeitgenössischen Musik. Hrsg. von Heinrich Lindlar.
Bonn: Boosey & Hawkes
1. Igor Strawinsky; zum siebzigsten Geburtstag. 1952.
2. Ballett-Heft. 1952.
3. Béla Bartók. 1953.
4. England-Heft. 1953.
5. Serge Prokofieff. 1953.
6. Oper im XX. Jahrhundert. 1954.

7. Benjamin Britten. 1954.
8. Tschechische Komponisten; Janáček, Martinů, Hâba, Weinberger. 1954.
9. Ungarische Komponisten. 1954.
10. Schweizer Komponisten; Bericht und Bekenntnis. 1955.
11. Benjamin Britten; das Opernwerk. 1955.
12. Strawinsky in Amerika; das kompositorische Werk von 1939 bis 1955. 1955.

Musik der Zeit; eine Schriftenreihe zur Musik und Gegen-
    wart. Neue Folge. Hrsg. von Heinrich Lindlar and Rein-
    hold Schubert.
Bonn: Boosey & Hawkes
1. Strawinsky; Wirklichkeit und Wirkung. 1958.
2. Die drei grossen "F"; Film - Funk - Fernsehen. 1958.
3. Lebt die Oper? 1960.

Die Musik im alten und neuen Europa. Hrsg. von Walter
    Wiora.
Kassel: J. P. Hinnenthal
1. Wiora, W. Europäische Volksmusik und abendländische
    Tonkunst. 1957.
2. Salmen, W. Die Schichtung der mittelalterlichen
    Musikkultur in der ostdeutschen Grenzlage. 1954.
3. Komma, K. Das Böhmische Musikantentum. 1960.
4. Salmen, W. Der fahrende Musiker im europäischen
    Mittelalter. 1960.

Musik und Zeit
Halle/Saale: Mitteldeutscher Verlag, No. 7 in Leipzig by
    Hofmeister
1. Die sowjetische Musik im Aufstieg; eine Sammlung von
    Aufsätzen. Hrsg. vom Sowjetischen Komponistenverband
    der UdSSR. Uebers. von Wolfram Sterz et al. 1952.
2. Um die Grundlagen der Musik; Diskussionsbeiträge
    über die Auswirkung der Arbeit J. W. Stalins "Der

Marxismus und die Fragen der Sprachwissenschaft" auf
die Musik. Uebers. von Wolfram & Karl Sterz et al.
Teil 1. 1952.
3. Schneerson, G. Musik im Dienste der Reaktion.
Uebers. von Doris Dauber. 1952.
4. Liwanowa, T. N. Die Kritikertätigkeit der russischen
klassischen Komponisten. Uebers. von G. Comte. Redaktion: Wolfram Sterz. 1953.
5. Gorodinski, W. Geistige Armut in der Musik. Uebers.
von Nikolai Rechn, Nelly Richter et al. Redaktion:
Wolfram Sterz. 1953.
6. Probleme der sowjetischen Musik; eine Sammlung von
Aufsätzen. Uebers. von Walter Dutz et al. Redaktion:
Wolfram & Karl Sterz. 1953.
7. Um die Grundlagen der Musik; Diskussionsbeiträge über
die Auswirkung der Arbeit J. W. Stalins "Der Marxismus
und die Fragen der Sprachwissenschaft" auf die Musik.
Uebers., Redaktion, & Vorwort von Wolfram und Karl
Sterz. Teil 2. 1954.
No more published.

Musikalische Gegenwartsfragen. Hrsg. von Heinrich
Besseler.
Heidelberg: Müller-Thiergarten
1. Besseler, H. Zum Problem der Tenorgeige. 1949.
2. Wiora, W. Das echte Volkslied. 1950.
3. Husmann, H. Vom Wesen der Konsonanz. 1953.

Musikalische Zeitfragen. Schriftenreihe, im Auftrag des
Deutschen Musikrates [der Deutschen Sektion des Internationalen Musikrates] hrsg. von Walter Wiora.
Kassel: Bärenreiter
1. Bonner Tagung, 1955. Neue Zusammenarbeit im deutschen
Musikleben; Vorträge und Entschliessungen der Bonner
Tagung 1955. 1956.
2. Musik im Wandel von Freizeit und Bildung. 1957.

3. Rundfunk und Hausmusik; Gegensatz oder Ergänzung? 1958.
4. Sass, H. , E. Kraus, H. Mersmann, & W. Wiora, ed. Der Deutsche Musikrat 1953-58. 1959.
5. Blume, F. Was ist Musik? Ein Vortrag. 1959.
6. Wiora, W. Komponist und Mitwelt.
7. Das Volkslied heute. 1959.
8. Mersmann, H. Freiheit und Bindung im künstlerischen Schaffen. 1960.
9. Die vielspältige Musik und die allgemeine Musiklehre. 1960.
10. Die Natur der Musik als Problem der Wissenschaft. 1962.
11. Sydow, K. , ed. Musik in Volksschule und Lehrerbildung; ein Tagungsbericht. 1961.
12. Křenek, E. Komponist und Hörer; ein Vortrag. 1964.

Musikalisches Brevier
Bielefeld: J. P. Hinnenthal. No. 1 unnumbered.
1. Schumann, R. Musikalische Haus- und Lebensregeln. 1947.
2. Wackenroder, W. H. Musikalische Schriften. Vorwort von Richard Benz. 1948.

Musik-Bibliotek
København: W. Hansen. Partly numbered.
1. Fischer, E. Musikalske betragtninger. Oversat af Jacob Paludan. 2. oplag. 1953.
2. ----. Johann Sebastian Bach; en studie. Oversat af Jacob Paludan.
3. Simonsen, R. Sub specie aeternitatis; musikkulturelle perspektiver. 1942.
4. Johnsson, B. Chopkins klavermusik; i anledning af 100-året for komponistens død. 1949.
5. Jeppesen, K. Kontrapunkt; Vokalpolyfoni.

6. Jacobsen, O. Klaverpaedagogik.

7. Malling, O. Instrumentationslaere. 6. oplag.

8. Ravn-Jonsen, J. Musikhistorier. Samlet af J. Ravn-Jonsen med tegninger af Vald. Møller.

9. Bohlmann, G. C. Kortfattet musikalsk lommeordbog.

10. Seligmann, H. Skikkelser i tonekunsten.

11. Meyer-Radon, W. Spaending og aispaending i klaverspillets teknik.

12. Tarp, S. E. Koralharmonisering i dur og mol; en kortfattet vejledning.

13/16. Wöldike, M., ed. Laerebog til brug for seminariernes musikundervisning.

13. Hefte 1. Ring, O. Melodilaere.

14. Hefte 2. Zacharias, A. Stemmedannelse.

15. Hefte 3. Emborg, J. L. Musikopdragelse i børneskolen.

16. Hefte 4. Hamburger, P. Musikens historie i omrids.

17. Lützhöft, O. Kortfattet musikteori til brug ved musik- og solfege-undervisningen.

18. Simonsen, R. Musikhistorisk kompendium; ledetråd ved musikpaedagogisk eksamen. 1946.

19. Gram, P. Musikens formlaere.

20. Høffding, F. Den elementaere hørelaere, til brug ved sangundervisning i skoler.

21. Henrichsen, R. Den musikalske ornamentik (forsiringslaeren).

22. Glass, L. Pedalens anvendelse ved klaverspillet.

23. Holm, I. 100 musikdiktater og en indledning om solfège.

24. Bang, P. Om sangundervisning.

25. Brems, A. Om tonedannelse.

26. Malko, N. The Conductor and His Baton; Fundamentals of the Technic of Conducting.

27. Flor, K. Johann Sebastian Bach; en biografi. 1950.

28. Johnsson, B. Musikkens stilarter. 1950.

29. Gide, A. Notater om Chopin; på dansk ved Tage Brüel.

30. Bentzon, N. V. Tolvtoneteknik. 1953.

31. ----. Seks monologer. 1954.

Musikbücherei für jedermann
Leipzig: Breitkopf und Härtel

1. Lewik, B. Franz Schubert; ein Vortrag. Uebers. von
   W. Biehahn. Hrsg. vom Deutschen Schubertausschuss.
   1953.

2. Remesow, I. Michail Iwanowitsch Glinka; ein Vortrag.
   Uebers. von E. M. Arndt. 1953.

3. Zeraschi, H. Das Orchester. 1954.

4. Schmitz, E. Das mächtige Häuflein [Modest Mussorgskij, Nicolai Rimskij-Korssakow, Alexander Borodin, César
   Cui und Mili Balakirew]. 1955.

5. Creuzburg, E. Robert Schumann. 1955.

6. Dehnert, M. Vom musikalischen Hören. 1955. 2.
   Auflage 1962.

7. Seifert, W. Giuseppe Verdi; eine Einführung in Leben
   und Werk. 1955.

8. Petzoldt, R. Wolfgang Amadeus Mozart; Leben und
   Werk. 1956.

9. Hoffmann, M. Gustav Albert Lortzing; der Meister der
   deutschen Volksoper. 1956.

10. Worbs, H. C. Felix Mendelssohn-Bartholdy. 1956.
    2. Auflage 1957.

11. Schulze, H. Antonín Dvořák. 1956.

12. Petzoldt, R. Die Oper in ihrer Zeit. 1956.

13. Benary, P. Anton Bruckner. 1956.

14. Seifert, W. Giacomo Puccini. 1957.

15. Schrammek, W. Ueber Ursprung und Anfänge der
    Musik. 1957.

16. Richter, H. Leoš Janáček. 1958.

17. Kroher, E. Impressionismus in der Musik. 1957.

18. Streller, F. Sergej Prokofjew. 1960.

19. Brockhaus, H. A. Hanns Eisler. 1961.

20. Seeger, H. Joseph Haydn. 1961.

21. Brockhaus, H. A. Dmitri Schostakowitsch. 1962.
In prep.

Becker, H. ABC der Musiktheorie.

Hofmann, H. P. Schlager-ABC.

Elsner, J. Fryderyk Chopin.

Dehnert, M. Richard Wagner.

Schmidt, E. Giuseppe Verdi.

Hennenberg, F. Paul Dessau.

Rebling, E. Ballett.

Köhler, S. Musik unserer Zeit.

Mlynarczyk, H. Die Violine und ihre Meister.

Braschowanowa, L. Kleine Geschichte der bulgarischen Musik.

Musiker, die der Welt gehören
London, Wien, Frankfurt: Joseph Weinberger
1. Jantsch, E. Friedrich Gulda; die Verantwortung des Interpreten. 1953.
No more published.

Musikerreihe
Olten (Schweiz): Walter
1. Cherbuliez, A. E. Johann Sebastian Bach; sein Leben und sein Werk. 1946.
2. Weingartner, C. Franz Schubert; sein Leben und sein Werk. 1947.
3. Orel, A. Johannes Brahms; ein Meister und sein Weg. 1948.
4. Reich, W. Richard Wagner; Leben, Fühlen, Schaffen. 1948.
5. Cherbuliez, A. E. Georg Friedrich Händel; Leben und Werk. 1949.
6. Redlich, H. F. Claudio Monteverdi; Leben und Werk. 1949.
7. Müller, E. Robert Schumann; eine Bildnisstudie. 1950.
8. Tappolet, W. Maurice Ravel; Leben und Werk. 1950.
9. Ringbom, N. E. Jan Sibelius; ein Meister und sein Werk. 1950.
10. Tenschert, R. Christoph Willibald Gluck; der grosse Reformator der Oper. 1951.
11. Zentner, W. Carl Maria von Weber; sein Leben und

sein Schaffen. 1952.

12. Kühner, H. Hector Berlioz; Charakter und Schöpfertum. 1952.

13. Erhardt, O. Richard Strauss; Leben, Wirken, Schaffen. 1953.

14. Pahlen, K. Manuel de Falla und die Musik in Spanien. 1954.

15. Ehinger, H. E. T. A. Hoffmann als Musiker und Musikschriftsteller. 1954.

No more published with numbers.

Der Musikfreund. Hrsg. von Franz Grasberger.

Wien: Kaltschmid

1. Griesinger, G. A. Biographische Notizen über Joseph Haydn. Mit einem Nachwort und Anmerkungen neu hrsg. von Franz Grasberger. 1954.

Musiknovellen. Für den Schulmusikunterricht. Hrsg. von Otto Daube.

Dortmund: Crüwell

1. Hoffmann, E. T. A. Ritter Gluck; eine Erinnerung aus dem Jahre 1809. 1961.

2. Daube, O. Der heilige Strom; Novellen und Szenen um Johann Sebastian Bach. 1961.

3. Mörike, E. F. Mozart auf der Reise nach Prag. 1961.

4. Wagner, R. Eine Pilgerfahrt zu Beethoven. 1961.

Musikpädagogische Bibliothek. Neue Folge. Hrsg. von Eberhard Preussner.

Heidelberg: Quelle & Meyer

1. Preussner, E. Allgemeine Musikerziehung. 1959.

2. Sachs, C. Vergleichende Musikwissenschaft; Musik der Fremdkulturen. 2., neubearb. Auflage 1959.

3. Bresgen, C. Die Improvisation. 1960.

4. Loebenstein, F. Klavierpädagogik. 2., neubearb. Auflage 1960.

5. Kolneder, W. Geschichte der Musik; ein Studien- und Prüfungshelfer. 1961.

6. Preussner, E. Wie studiere ich Musik? Ein Ratgeber. 1962.

7. Kolneder, W. Musikinstrumentenkunde; ein Studien- und Prüfungshelfer. 1963.

In prep.

    Fischer-Junghann, E. Gesangsbildungslehre.

    Stoverock, D. Gehörbildung.

    Thiel, J. Die technischen Hilfsmittel im Musikunterricht.

Musikschulwerk

Leipzig: Hofmeister

1. Bimberg, S., C. Lange, & F. Bachmann. Vom Singen zum Musikverstehen; Musikmethodik. Lehrbuch für den Musikunterricht in Schulen und Volkskunstgruppen. Neudruck. 1962.

Musikwissenschaft. Hrsg. von Gottfried Schmid.

Zürich: Mondial Verlag

1. Scherchen, H. Vom Wesen der Musik. Band 1: Das moderne Musikempfinden. 1946.

Musikwissenschaftliche Arbeiten. Hrsg. von der Gesellschaft für Musikforschung.

Kassel: Bärenreiter

1. Blume, F. Johann Sebastian Bach im Wandel der Geschichte. 1947.

2. Lipphardt, W. Die Weisen der lateinischen Osterspiele des 12. und 13. Jahrhunderts. 1948.

3. Dräger, H.H. Prinzip einer Systematik der Musikinstrumente. 1948.

4. Gerhardt, C. Die Torgauer Walter-Handschriften. 1949.

5. Walker, D.P. Der musikalische Humanismus im 16. und frühen 17. Jahrhundert. 1950.

6. Becker-Glauch, I. Die Bedeutung der Musik für die Dresdener Hoffeste bis in die Zeit Augusts des Starken 1951.

7. Moser, H. J. Das musikalische Denkmälerwesen in Deutschland. 1952.

8. Schmitz, H.-P. Die Tontechnik des Père Engramelle; ein Beitrag zur Lehre von der musikalischen Vortragskunst im 18. Jahrhundert. 1953.

9. King, A. H. Mozart im Spiegel der Geschichte, 1756-1956; eine kritische und bibliographische Studie. Uebers. von Bruno Grusnick. 1956.

10. Albrecht, H., ed. Die Bedeutung der Zeichen Keil, Strich und Punkt bei Mozart; fünf Lösungen einer Preisfrage. Im Auftrag der Gesellschaft für Musikforschung. 1957.

11. Braun, G. Die Schulmusikerziehung in Preussen von den Falkschen Bestimmungen zur Kestenberg-Reform. 1957.

12. Beyer, P. Studien zur Vorgeschichte des Dur-moll. 1958.

13. Krüger, W. Die authentische Klangform des primitiven organum. 1958.

14. Engelbrecht, C. Die Kasseler Hofkapelle im 17. Jahrhundert und ihre anonymen Musikhandschriften aus der Kasseler Landesbibliothek. 1958.

15. Schneider, M. Singende Steine. 1955.

16. Zenck, H. Numerus und Affectus; Studien zur Musikgeschichte. 1959.

17. Unverricht, H. Die Eigenschriften und die Originalausgaben von Werken Beethovens in ihrer Bedeutung für die moderne Textkritik. 1960.

18. Kirchner, G. Der Generalbass bei Heinrich Schütz. 1960.

19. Schaal, R. Verzeichnis deutschsprachiger musikwissenschaftlicher Dissertationen 1861-1960. 1963.

20. Pohlmann, H. Die Frühgeschichte des musikalischen

Urheberrechts (ca. 1400-1800). 1962.

Musikwissenschaftliche Einzeldarstellungen
Leipzig: Breitkopf und Härtel
1. Brock, H. Musiktheater in der Schule; eine Drama-
turgie der Schuloper. 1960.
2. Michel, P. Ueber musikalische Fähigkeiten und Fertig-
keiten; ein Beitrag zur Musikpsychologie. 1960.
Neudruck 1962.
3. Bachmann, W. Die Anfänge des Streichinstrumenten-
spiels. 1964.
4. Bimberg, S. Ueber das musikalische Hören. In prep.

Musikwissenschaftliche Reihe im Voggenreiter Verlag
Bad Godesberg: Voggenreiter
1. König, H. Rote Sterne glühn; Lieder im Dienste der
Sowjetisierung. 1955.

Musikwissenschaftliche Studienbibliothek. Hrsg. von Friedrich Gennrich.
Darmstadt: (Vols. 20/: Langen bei Frankfurt am Main):
F. Gennrich. All vols. by or ed. by F. Gennrich.
Partly music.
1/2. Abriss der frankonischen Mensuralnotation nebst
Uebertragungsmaterial. 2. Aufl. 1956.
3/4. Abriss der Mensuralnotation des XIV. und der
ersten Hälfte des XV. Jahrhunderts nebst Uebertragungsmaterial. 1948.
5/6. Die Sankt Viktor-Clausulae und ihre Motetten (Paris,
Bibl. Nat., Mss lat. 15139). 1953.
7. Aus der Formenwelt des Mittelalters. 1953.
8. Uebertragungsmaterial zur "Rhythmik der Ars antiqua."
1954.
9. Melodien altdeutscher Lieder. 1954.
10. Mittelhochdeutsche Liedkunst. 1954.
11. Lateinische Liedkontrafaktur; eine Auswahl lateinischer

Conductus mit ihren volkssprachigen Vorbildern. 1956.

12. Perotinus Magnus. Das Organum: Alleluia Nativitas gloriose virginis Marie und seine Sippe. 1955.

13/14. Musica sine Littera; Notenzeichen und Rhythmik der Gruppennotation. 1956.

15/16. Franco de Colonia. Magistri Franconis Ars Cantus Mensurabilis. 1957.

17. Exempla altfranzösischer Lyrik. 1958.

18/19. Lo Gai Saber; 50 ausgewählte Troubadour-Lieder, Melodie, Text, Kommentar, Formenlehre und Glossar. 1959.

20. Adam de la Halle. Le Jeu de Robin et de Marion; Li Rondel Adam. 1962.

21. Die autochthone Melodie. 1963.

De Muziek

's-Gravenhage: J. P. Kruseman

1. Göllerich, A. Beethoven. Met een inleiding van Richard Strauss. 1930.

2. Pembaur, J. De Poëzie van het klavierspel.

3. Dalen, H. van. Moussorgsky. 1930.

4. Balfoort, D. Eigenartige musikinstrumente.

5. Sollitt, E. Mengelberg spreekt. 1936?

6. Hutschenruyter, W. , & P. Kruseman. Musiciana. 1938?

7. Bigot, L. C. T. Wonderkinderen. 1938?

8. Couturier, L. Dirigenten van dezen tijd. 1938?

9. Flothuis, M. Mozart. 1940.

10. Hutschenruyter, W. Chopin; zijn leven en werken. 1938?

11. Coster, D. Muziek in woorden. 1938?

12. Zagwijn, H. Debussy. 1940.

13. Hutschenruyter, W. Een bloemlezing uit de brieven van Beethoven. 1939.

14. Gilbert, W. G. , & C. Poustochkine. Jazzmuziek. 1939.

15. Prick van Wely, M. Over de piano en de pianomuziek.

1942.

16. Prick van Wely, M., & H. Huls. Over het orgel en de orgelmuziek. 1943.

17. Gilbert, W. G. Muziek uit oost en west; inleiding tot de inheemsche muziek van Nederlandsch Oost en West-Indië. 1942?

18. Hutschenruyter, W. Franz Schubert; zijn leven en werke. 1944?

19. Gilbert, W. G. Rumbamuziek; volksmuziek van de Midden-Amerikaansche Negers. 1945?

20. Triebels, H. Spaanse componisten van de laatste honderd jaar. 195-.

Muziek-paedagogische bibliotheek. Onder leiding van Willem Gehrels.
Purmerend: J. Muusses

1. Langelaar, A. Voorbereidend muziekonderwijs, op grondslag van de methode voor A. V. M. O. van Willem Gehrels. 1954.

2. Westera, A. Psalm en lied op de Christelijke scholen in verband met de methode Gehrels. 1954.

3. Bos, C. Muzikale improvisatie. 1955.

4. Gehrels, W. De volksmuziekschool. 1957.

5. Schijve, C. Eerst doen, dan praten. 1960.

National School Brass Band Association Handbooks
London: Hinrichsen

1. Cook, K., & L. Caisley. Music Through the Brass Band. Foreword by Eric Ball. 1953.
   Further vols. in prep.

Neue Studien zur Musikwissenschaft. Hrsg. von der Kommission für Musikwissenschaft der Akademie der Wissenschaften und der Literatur.
Mainz: Schott

1. Schmitz, A. Die Bildlichkeit der wortgebundenen

Musik Johann Sebastian Bachs. 1950.

2. Jammers, E. Der mittelalterliche Choral; Art und Herkunft. 1954.

3. Gurlitt, W. Die Epochengliederung der Musikgeschichte nach musikalisch-rhythmischen Prinzipien. In prep.

Neujahrsblatt der Allgemeinen Musikgesellschaft Zürich
Zürich: Hug in Kommission

133/134. Fehr, M., P. Sieber, & G. Walter, ed. Zürichs musikalische Vergangenheit im Bild. 1945.

135/137. Kirchner, T. Briefe aus den Jahren 1860-68, ausgewählt und mit einer Einführung versehen von Peter Otto Schneider. 1949.

138. Refardt, E. Der "Goethe-Kayser," ein Nachklang zum Goethejahr 1949. 1950.

139. Freund, R. Memoiren eines Pianisten. 1951.

140. Caflisch, L., & M. Fehr. Der junge Mozart in Zürich. 1952.

141. Fehr, M. Musikalische Jagd. 1954.

142. Schnyder von Wartensee, X. Xaver Schnyder von Wartensee und Hans Georg Nägeli; Briefe aus den Jahren 1811 bis 1821. Ausgewählt von Peter Otto Schneider. 1955.

143. Giegling, F. Volkmar Andreae. Mit einem Beitrag von Leopold Nowak. 1959.

144. Reimann, H. Huldrych Zwingli, der Musiker. 1960.

145. Briner, A., & F. Jakob. Das Musikbild und die Hausorgel im Landgut "Zur Schipf" in Herrliberg-Zürich. 1961.

146. Schnyder von Wartensee, X. Xaver Schnyder von Wartensee und Hans Georg Nägeli; Briefe aus den Jahren 1822 bis 1835. Ausgewählt von Peter Otto Schneider. 1962.

147. Jakob, F. Paul Müller; Biographie und Werkverzeichnis. 1963.

148. Cherbuliez, A.-E. Johann Ludwig Steiner; Stadttrompe-

ter von Zürich. 1964.

The Neujahrsblätter for 1812-1899 are indexed in Nos. 140 (1952) and 141 (1954).

The Neujahrsblätter for 1900-50 are indexed in No. 139 (1951)

Novello's Music Primers

London: Novello. Nos. 1-121 appeared before 1945.

122. Anson, H. V. Extempore Pianoforte Accompaniment. 1951.

123. Lang, C. S. 100 Score Reading Exercises in G and F Clefs. Book I (A. R. C. O. standard).

124. ----. 100 Score Reading Exercises in G, F and C Clefs. Book II (F. R. C. O. standard).

125. ----. Harmonic and Melodic Dictation Tests. Book I (A. R. C. O. standard).

126. ----. Harmonic and Melodic Dictation Tests. Book II (F. R. C. O. standard).

127. ----. Melodies and Basses, to be harmonized in four parts at the keyboard (F. R. C. O. standard).

128. ----. Exercises for Organists. Book I (A. R. C. O. standard) . 1952.

129. ----. Exercises for Organists. Book II (F. R. C. O. standard). 1952.

130. Cole, W. The Rudiments of Music. 1952.

131. Hollinrake, H. Foundations of Harmony for Class-Teaching. 1954.

132. Cole, W. Questions on the Rudiments of Music.

133. Eldridge, G. Exercises in Playing from Three-Part Vocal Score.

134. Cleall, C. Voice Production in Choral Technique. 1955.

135. Thiman, E. Improvisation on Hymn Tunes.

136. Lang, C. S. Paper-Work Tests (A. R. C. O. standard). 1954.

137. ----. Paper-Work Tests (F. R. C. O. standard). 1955.

138. Eele, M. Listening Together (Teacher's Book).
139. ----. Listening Together (Pupil's Book).
140. Judd, P. Musicianship for Singers. 1957.
141. Saunders, R. The Flute.
142. Lang, C. S. Harmony at the Keyboard. 1959.
143. Firth, W. Class Singing and Aural Training in the Junior School.
144. Brydson, J. Phrasing; Graded Exercises With Study Notes. 1961.
145. Milner, A. Harmony for Class Teaching. Book I.
146. ----. Harmony for Class Teaching. Book II.

Nueva visión; Música
Buenos Aires: Editorial Nueva Visión
5. Paz, J. C. Arnold Schönberg; o, el fin de la era tonal. 1958.

Opera Pocket Books
London: Black
1. Cochrane, P. , & Q. Chavez. Madame Butterfly. 1962.
2. ----. The Marriage of Figaro. 1962.

Operní libreta Antonína Dvořáka
Praha: SNKLHU
1. Dvořák, A. Král a uhlíř. Kritické vyd. připravil Jarmil Burghauser. 1957.

Organik
Wolfenbüttel: Möseler
1. Jöde, F. Die Kunst Bachs, dargestellt an seinen Inventionen. 1926. Unveränd. Neuaufl. anlässlich des 70. Geburtstages des Verfasser. 1957.

Die Orgel-Monographien
Mainz: Rheingold-Verlag
1. Stahl, W. Die "Totentanz"-Orgel der Marienkirche in

131

Lübeck. Mainz: P. Smets, 1932. 2. Auflage, Rheingold, 1942.

2. Wörsching, J. Die Orgelwerke der Abtei Ottobeuren. 2. Auflage, neu bearbeitet von Paul Smets. Also available in English under the title: The Ottobeuren Abbey's Organs.

3. Raugel, F.   Die Domorgel von Toul. Uebersetzung aus dem Französischen von Paul Smets. 1932. 2. Auflage 1939. 3. Auflage 1946.

4. ----. Die Orgelwerke der Abtei St.-Mihiel. Uebersetzung aus dem Französischen von Paul Smets. 1933. 2. Auflage 1939. 3. Auflage 1946.

5. Spies, H. Abt Vogler und die von ihm 1805 simplifizierte Orgel von St. Peter in Salzburg. 1932. 3. Auflage 1947.

6. Smets, P. Die Orgel der St. Valentinuskirche zu Kiedrich. 1945.

7. Moore, T. Die Orgel der Christus-Kathedrale in Liverpool. Aus dem Englischen übersetzt von Paul Smets. 1934. 2. Aufl. 1945.

8. Freeman, A., & H. Willis. Die Orgelwerke der St. Pauls-Kathedrale zu London. Aus dem Englischen übersetzt von Paul Smets. 1945.

9. Smets, P. Die grosse Gabler-Orgel der Abtei Weingarten. 1940.

10. Wörsching, J. Die Orgelwerke der Abteien Maursmünster und Ebersmünster, mit Beiträgen von Marcel Thomann und Paul Smets. 1956.

11. Smets, P. Die berühmten Orgelwerke der Stadt Lübeck. 1945.

12. Lunelli, R. Die Orgelwerke von S. Marco in Venedig. 1957.

13. ----. Die Orgelwerke von S. Petronio zu Bologna. 1956.

14. Heiling, H. Die Orgelwerke der Stiftskirche zu Herzogenburg und der Michaelerkirche zu Wien. 1958.

15. Wörsching, J. Die grosse Orgel der Kathedrale zu Reims. 1946.

16. ----. Die Compenius-Orgel auf Schloss Frederiksborg, Kopenhagen. 1946.

17. Lunelli, R. Die Orgelwerke von San Giovanni de Laterano und des Päpstlichen Institutes für Kirchenmusik in Rom.

18. Haupt, R. Die Orgel von St. Sixtus zu Northeim.

19. Pfeiffer-Dürkop, H. Die Geschichte der Gottfried-Fritzsche-Orgel in St. Katharinen zu Braunschweig. 1956.

20. Quoika, R. Die grosse Orgel des Abbate Franz Xaver Chrismann in St. Florian. 1948.

21. Wörsching, J. Die Orgelwerke des Münsters zu Strassburg i. E. 1947.

22. Silva y Ramón, G. Die Orgelwerke der Kathedrale zu Sevilla. Aus dem Spanischen übersetzt von Paul Smets. 2. Auflage 1947.

23. Lunelli, R. Die Orgel in der Kirche des Ritterordens vom Hl. Stephan zu Pisa. 1956.

24. ----. Die Orgelwerke von S. Guiseppe und S. Maria Rotonda zu Brescia. 1956.

25. Wörsching, J. Die Kemper-Orgel in der Kirche des Evang. Johannes-Stiftes zu Berlin-Spandau.

26. Lunelli, R. Die Orgelwerke des Domes zu Mailand und der Kathedrale zu Messina. 1947.

27. ----. Die Orgelwerke von S. Maria del Fiore in Florenz. 1956.

28. ----. Die Orgelwerke von S. Maria Maggiore zu Trient. 1957.

29. Quoika, R. Die Orgel von St. Mauritius in Olmütz.

30. Lunelli, R. Die Orgel von S. Nicolo l'Arena zu Catania. 1956.

31. Scheuermann, G. Die Orgelwerke von St. Elisabeth zu Breslau. 1958.

32. Heiling, H. Die Festorgel der Stiftskirche zu Kloster-

neuburg bei Wien. 1958.

33. Lunelli, R. Die Orgelwerke von S. Pietro in Trapani und S. Martino delle Scale bei Palermo. 1956.

34. Heiling, H. Die Orgel der Franziskanerkirche zu Wien. 1958.

35. Quoika, R. Die Orgel der Teinkirche zu Prag.

36. Lunelli, R. Die Orgel von S. Maria Assunta in Carignano zu Genua. 1956.

40. ----. Die Orgelwerke der Abtei Montecassino. 1956.

43. ----. Die Orgelwerke der Kathedrale zu Cremona. 1956.

46. Heiling, H. Die Orgel der Stiftskirche zu Heiligenkreuz bei Wien. 1959.

48. Winter, C. Die grosse Orgel im Münster zu Freiburg im Breisgau.

49. Heiling, H. Johann Ignaz Egedacher und seine Orgel in der Stiftskirche zu Zwettl in Niederösterreich. 1959.

58. Wörsching, J. Die Silbermann-Orgel im Dome zu Freiberg (Sachsen).

60. David, W. Die Orgel von St. Marien zu Berlin und andere berühmte Berliner Orgeln. 1949.

Orgelwissenschaftliche Arbeits- und Musikgemeinschaft.
Rundbrief.
Hillerse 70 über Northeim (Han): Rudolf Haupt

1. Haupt, R. Zur Situation der Orgel in Deutschland. 1953.

2. ----. Die Orgel im evangelischen Kultraum in Geschichte und Gegenwart. 1954.

Orgues d'Alsace
Strasbourg: Éditions Europea

2. Bender, A. Les orgues Silbermann de Marmoutier et Ebermunster. Avec la collaboration de Marcel Thomann. 1960.

Orpheus-Bücher. Hrsg. von F. Racek.

Wien: Brüder Hollinek
1. Orel, A. Hugo Wolf; ein Künstlerbildnis. 1947.
2. Brauner, R. F. Oesterreichs neue Musik; ein Wegweiser und Ueberblick für den Musikfreund. 1948.
3. Burney, C. Dr. Charles Burney's Musikalische Reise durch das alte Oesterreich (1772), neu hrsg. und eingeleitet von Bernhard Paumgartner. 1948.
4. Křenek, E. Musik im goldenen Westen; das Tonschaffen der USA. 1949.
5. Tenschert, R. Richard Strauss und Wien; eine Wahlverwandtschaft. 1949.
6-7. Preussner, E. Musikgeschichte des Abendlandes; eine Betrachtung für der Musikliebhaber. 2 Bd. 1951.
8. Schubert, F. P. Franz Schubert; Briefe und Schriften. 4. verm. und erläuterte Ausgabe, hrsg. von Otto Erich Deutsch. 1954.

Orpheus-Schriftenreihe zu Grundfragen der Musik. Hrsg. von der Gesellschaft zur Förderung der Systematischen Musikwissenschaft, Düsseldorf.
Düsseldorf: Gesellschaft zur Förderung der Systematischen Musikwissenschaft; Frankfurt/Main: Verlag Das Musikinstrument in Kommission
1. Vogel, M. Die Intonation der Blechbläser; neue Wege im Metallblas-Instrumentenbau. 1961.
2. ----. Der Tristan-Akkord und die Krise der modernen Harmonielehre. 1962.
3-4. Die Enharmonik der Griechen. Teil 1: Tonsystem und Notation. Teil 2: Der Ursprung der Enharmonik. 1963.

Pamphlet Series; Pamfletreeks. Published by The South African Society of Music Teachers; Die Suid-Afrikaanse Vereniging van Musiekonderwysers, Capetown.
2. South African Society of Music Teachers. Collected Conference Addresses; Versamelde konferensie-toesprake, 1955-1956-1957 at Pietermaritzburg, Stellenbosch, Johan-

nesburg. Ed. by M. E. de Graaf. 195-.
No more published.

Pan American Music Series
Washington, D. C. : Division of Music and Visual Arts,
   Department of Cultural Affairs, Pan American Union
1. Chase, G. Partial List of Latin American Music Obtainable in the United States. With a supplementary list
   of books and a selective list of phonograph records.
   1941. 2nd ed. 1942.
      Thompson, L. (Fern). Partial List of Latin American
   Music Obtainable in the United States. 3rd ed. , rev. and
   enl. 1948.
2. Historical Records Survey, District of Columbia. Bio-
   Bibliographical Index of Musicians in the United States
   of America From Colonial Times. Prepared by the District of Columbia Historical Records Survey. Planned in
   1936 by Keyes Porter; revived and expanded in 1940 under
   the supervision of Leonard Ellinwood. 1941. 2nd ed.
   1956.
3. Durán, G. Recordings of Latin American Songs and
   Dances; An Annotated Selected List of Popular and Folk
   Music. Sponsored by National Bureau for the Advance-
   ment of Music and National and Inter-American Music
   Week Committee. 1942. 2nd ed. , rev. and enl. by Gilbert Chase, 1950.
4. ----. 14 Traditional Spanish Songs from Texas, tran-
   scribed by Gustavo Durán from recordings made in
   Texas, 1934-39, by John A. , Ruby T. and Alan Lomax.
   1942.
5. Luper, A. T. The Music of Argentina. 1942.
6. Pereira Salas, E. Notes on the History of Music Exchange Between the Americas Before 1940. A trans. of
   Notas para la historia del intercambio musical entre las
   Américas by Eugenio Pereira Salas. 1943.
7. ----. Notas para la historia del intercambio musical

entre las Américas antes del año 1940. 1943.

8. Brooks, C. Opportunities for Advanced Study of Music in the United States; A Classified Index of Courses in Music Offered by Universities, Colleges, Music Schools, and Conservatories in the Academic year 1941-42. 1943.

9. Luper, A. T. The Music of Brazil. 1943.

10. Pan American Union, Division of Music and Visual Arts. Carlos Chávez; Catalog of His Works. Preface by Herbert Weinstock. 1944.

11. Salas Viu, V. Músicos modernos de Chile. 1944.

12. Lawler, V, Educación musical en 14 repúblicas americanas; Music Education in 14 American Republics. 1945.

13. Thompson, L. (Fern). Selected References in English on Latin American Music; A Reading List Compiled and Annotated by Leila Fern. 1944.

14. Mayer-Serra, O. El estado presente de la música en Mexico; The Present State of Music in Mexico. 1946.

15. Coopersmith, J. M. Music and Musicians of the Dominican Republic; Música y músicos de la República Dominicana. Trad. por Maria Hazera y Elizabeth M. Tylor. 1949.

16. Corrêa de Azevedo, L. H. A música brasileira e seus fundamentos; Brief History of Music in Brazil. Trans. into English by Elizabeth M. Tylor and Mercedes de Moura Reis. 1948.

No more published.

Państwowa Wyższa Szkoła Muzyczna w Katowicach [Katowice, Poland]. Biblioteka. Katalogi.

1-2. Katalog książek zagranicznych. Nowe nabytki I. 1962. II. 1963.

3. Katalog dubletów; Catalogue of Music-Books, Printed Music and Periodicals for Exchange. 1962.

----. Biblioteka. Prace Biblioteki.

1. Musioł, K. Biblioteka Państwowej Wyższej Szkoły Muzycznej w Katowicach; The Library of the Higher School of Music in Katowice. 1960.

2. ----. Biblioteki muzyczne Austrii; les bibliothèques musicales en Austriche. 1959.

3. ----. Chopiniana w Bibliotece Państwowej Wyższej Szkoły Muzycznej w Katowicach; Chopiniana in the High Music School Library in Katowice. 1961.

4. Przystaś, C. Bibliografia polskich śpiewników szkolnych. In prep.

7. Opracowanie rzeczowe zbiorów muzycznych. In prep.

8. Musioł, K. Organizacja i inwentaryzacja zbiorów muzycznych; Organisation et inventaire des fonds musicaux. 1961.

----. Biblioteka. Wykłady i prelekcje.

1. Niemand, S. Enrico Caruso, 1873-1921. 1961.

2. Szalonek, W. Claude Debussy. 1962.

3. Bogusławski, E. , & Z. Kocielski. Formy artystycznej muzyki Orientu. In prep.

4. Świder, J. Arnold Schönberg, 1874-1951. 1962.

5. Habela, J. Zagadnienie reformy tradycyjnej notacji muzycznej; Das Problem der Reform der traditionellen Notenschrift. 1963.

----. Lektorat języka niemieckiego. Przekłady.

1. Weingartner, F. O dyrygowaniu. 1961.

2. Busoni, F. Zarys nowej estetyki muzyki. 1962.

3. Grube, M. L. Problemy gry skrzypcowej. 1963.

4. Schumann, R. O twórczości Fr. Chopina. In prep.

5. Huberman, B. Z warsztatu wirtuoza. In prep.

Papers of the Hymn Society of America [formerly Hymn Society]
New York: Hymn Society of America

1. Benson, L. F. The Hymns of John Bunyan. 1930.

2. Merrill, W. P. The Religious Value of Hymns. 1931.
3. Messenger, R. E. The Praise of the Virgin in Early Latin Hymns. 1932.
4. Pratt, *N.* S. The Significance of the Old French Psalter. 1933.
5. Hymn Society, N. Y. Hymn Festival Programs. 1934.
6. Price, C. F. What Is a Hymn? 1937.
7. Foote, H. W. An Account of the Bay Psalm Book. 1940.
8. Mason, H. L. Lowell Mason; An Appreciation of His Life and Work. 1941.
9. Messenger, R. E. Christian Hymns of the First Three Centuries. 1942.
10. Hymn Society of America. Addresses at the 20th Anniversary of the Hymn Society of America. 1943.
11. ----. Twelve New Hymns of Christian Patriotism. 1945.
12. Reed, L. D. Luther and Congregational Song. 1947.
13. Hope, N. V. Isaac Watts and His Contribution to English Hymnody. 1947.
14. Messenger, R. E. Latin Hymns of the Middle Ages. 1948.
15. Higginson, J. V. Revival of Gregorian Chant; Its Effect on English Hymnody. 1949.
16. McAll, R. L. The Hymn Festival Movement in America; A Handbook for Hymn Festivals. 1951.
17. Foote, H. W. Recent American Hymnody. 1952.
18. Higginson, J. V. The American Indians and Hymnody. 1954.
19. Noyes, M. P. Louis F. Benson, Hymnologist. 1955.
20. Johansen, J. H. The Olney Hymns. 1956.
21. Thomas, N. W. The Philosophy of the Hymn. 1956.
22. Haas, A. B. Charles Wesley. 1957.
23. Ellinwood, L. , & A. W. Douglas. Charles Winfred Douglas. 1958. Incl. a list of 1,000 titles in the Douglas Collection in the Washington Cathedral Library.
24. International Hymnological Conference, 2nd. Addresses

at the International Hymnological Conference, September 10-11, 1961, New York City. 1962.

Pechan-Reihe; Musiker-Portraits

Wien, München: Adalbert Pechan. All vols. by Hannes Gall.

1050. Johann Sebastian Bach. 1952.
1051. Georg Friedrich Haendel. 1952.
1052. Christoph Willibald Ritter Gluck. 1952.
1053. Franz Joseph Haydn. 1952.
1054. Wolfgang Amadeus Mozart. 1953.
1055. Ludwig van Beethoven. 1954.
1056. Carl Maria von Weber.
1057. Franz Schubert.
1058. Robert Schumann.
1059. Felix Mendelssohn-Bartholdy.
1060. Frederic Chopin.
1061. Hector Berlioz.
1062. Franz Liszt.
1063. Richard Wagner.
1064. Anton Bruckner.
1065. Hugo Wolf.
1066. Johannes Brahms.
1067. Josef Lanner.
1068. Johann Strauss.
1069. Gustav Mahler.
1070. Max Reger.
1071. Hans Pfitzner.
1072. Richard Strauss.
1073. Franz Schmidt.
1074. Joseph Marx.
1075. Wilhelm Kienzl.

The appearance of 1056-1075 unverified.

Phoenix Music Guides

London: Phoenix House

1. Young, P. M. Concerto. 1957.

2. Young, P. M. Symphony. 1957.

Piccola biblioteca Ricordi (P. B. R.)
Milano: Ricordi
1. Leydi, R. Eroi e fuorilegge nella ballata popolare americana. 1958.
2. Mancini, G. Breve storia della sinfonia. 1958.
3. Paliotti, V. Storia della Canzone napoletana. 1958.
4. Franchini, V. Il jazz; la tradizione. 1958.
5. Malipiero, G. F. Antonio Vivaldi; il prete rosso. 1958.
6. Pestalozza, L. La scuola nazionale russa. 1958.
7. Tintori, G. L'opera napoletana. 1959.
8. Castiglioni, N. Il linguaggio musicale dal rinascimento a oggi. 1959.
9. Allorto, R. Piccola storia della musica. 1959.
10. Montani, P. Viaggio intorno al pianoforte. 1959.
11. Codignola, M. Arte e magià di Nicolò Paganini. 1960.
12. Marchioro, G. Momenti e aspetti della messainscena. 1960.
13. Franchini, V. L'era dello swing. 1960.
14. Ortiz Oderigo, N. Dizionario del jazz. 1961.
15. Malipiero, R. Guida alla dodecafonia. 1961.
16. Polillo, A. Il jazz di oggi. 1961.
17. Machabey, A. La notazione musicale. Trad. di Giampiero Tintori. 1963.
18. Prevignano-Rapetti, I. Io, la canzone. 1962.
19. Bortolotto, M. Introduzione al lied romantico. 1962.
20. Haskell, A. Il balletto. 1962.
21. Pincherle, M. L'orchestra da camera. Trad. di Lily e Riccardo Allorto. 1963.
    Machabey, A. Il bel canto. In prep.
    Berio, L. La musica elettronica. In prep.

Pour la musique. Colletion dirigée par Roland-Manuel.
Paris: Gallimard. Partly numbered.
1. Barraud, H. La France et la musique occidentale.

1956.

2. Beaufils, M. Le lied romantique allemand. 1956.
3. Hahn, R. Du chant. 1957.
4. Samson, J. Musique et chant sacrês.
5. Dent, E. J. Les opéras de Mozart. 1958.
6. Einstein, A. La musique romantique. 1959.
7. Corbin, S. L'église à la conquête de sa musique.
1960.
   Haraszti, É. La danse et le ballet.
   Lesure, F. La musique de la renaissance en France
et les poètes.

Práce ze Semináře hudební výchovy na Masarykově Univer-
   sitě v Brně.
Řídí Bohumir Štědroň.
Praha: Hudební Matice Umělecké Besedy
   1. Helfert, V. O Janáčkovi; soubor statí a článků. 1949.
   2. ----. O Smetanovi; soubor statí a článků. 1950.

Publications de la Sociéte Belge de Musicologie; Uitgaven
   van de Belgische Vereeniging voor Muziekwetenschap
Série 1
   1. Collaer, P. Darius Milhaud. (Bibliothèque d'études
   musicales). Anvers: Nederlandsche Boekhandel, 1947.
Série 2
   1. Clercx, S. Le baroque et la musique; essai d'esthétique musicale.
      Bruxelles: Éd. de la Librairie Encyclopédique, 1948.
   2. Ackere, J. van. Pelléas et Mélisande. Bruxelles, 1952.

Publications de la Société Française de Musicologie
Paris: E. Droz (Série 2, T. 1-8), Heugel (S. 2, T. 9-10),
   Fishbacher (S. 3, T. 1)
Série 1: Monuments de la musique ancienne. Outside the
   scope of this study.
Série 2: Documents et catalogues

142

1-2. La Laurencie, L. de. Inventaire du fonds Blancheton de la Bibliothèque du Conservatoire de Musique de Paris (Symphonies du milieu du XVIIIe siècle), publié avec l'-incipit et le tableau de la composition thématique de chaque symphonie. 1930 & 1931.

3-4. Mélanges offerts à M. Lionel de la Laurencie. 1932 & 1933.

5-6. Dufourcq, N. Documents inédits relatifs à l'orgue français, extraits des archives et des bibliothèques (XIVe-XVIIIe siècles), publiés avec une introduction et des notes par N. Dufourcq. 1934 & 1935.

7. La Laurencie, L. de, & A. Gastoué. Catalogue des livres de musique (manuscrits et imprimés) de la Bibliothèque de l'Arsenal, à Paris. 1936.

8. Thibault, G., & L. Perceau. Bibliographie des poésies de P. de Ronsard mises en musique au XVIe siècle. 1942.

9. Lesure, F., & G. Thibault. Bibliographie des éditions d'Adrian Le Roy et Robert Ballard (1551-1598). 1955.

10. Briquet, M. La musique dans les congrès internationaux (1835-1939). 1961.

Série 3: Études

1. Rollin, J. Les chansons de Clément Marot; étude historique et bibliographique. 1951.

Publikationen der Schweizerischen Musikforschenden Gesellschaft. Serie 2.

Bern: Paul Haupt

1. Geering, A. Die Organa und mehrstimmigen Conductus in den Handschriften des deutschen Sprachgebietes vom 13. bis 16. Jahrhundert. 1952.

2. Schanzlin, H. P. Johann Melchior Gletles Motetten; ein Beitrag zur schweizerischen Musikgeschichte des 17. Jahrhunderts. 1954.

3. Internationaler Kongress für Kirchenmusik, Bern. Bericht über den internationalen Kongress für Kirchen-

musik in Bern 30. August bis 4. September 1952. 1953.

4. Oesch, H. Guido von Arezzo; Biographisches und Theoretisches unter besonderer Berücksichtigung der sogenannten odonischen Traktate. 1954.

5. Fischer, K. von. Studien zur italienischen Musik des Trecento und frühen Quattrocento; Tabellarischer Werkkatalog über das Quellenmaterial mit Anhang. 1956.

6. Refardt, E. Thematischer Katalog der Instrumentalmusik des 18. Jahrhunderts in den Handschriften der Universitätsbibliothek Basel. 1957.

7. Taling-Hajnali, M. Der fugierte Stil bei Mozart. 1959.

8. Labhardt, F. Das Sequentiar Cod. 546 der Stiftsbibliothek von St. Gallen und seine Quellen. 1959. Teil 2: Notenband. 1963.

9. Oesch, H. Berno und Hermann von Reichenau als Musiktheoretiker; mit einem Ueberblick über ihr Leben und die handschriftliche Ueberlieferung ihrer Werke. Beigabe: Das Geschichtswerk Hermanns des Lahmen in seiner Ueberlieferung, von Arno Duch. 1961.

10. Gullo, S. Das Tempo in der Musik des 13. und 14. Jahrhunderts. 1964.

11. 2. Internationaler Kongres für Kirchenmusik, Bern, 1962. Kirchenmusik in ökumenischer Schau. 1964.

Publikationer utg. av Kungl. Musikaliska Akademien med Musikhögskolan
Stockholm: Nordiska Musikförlaget

1. Wallner, B. Det musikaliska formstudiet. 1957.

2. Franzén, B. Att bedöma musikelever. 1959.

3. Edlund, L. Om gehörsutbildning. 1963.

Publikationer utg. av Kungl. Musikaliska Akademiens Biblioteket; Publications of the Library of the Royal Swedish Academy of Music
Stockholm: Kungl. Musikaliska Akademiens Biblioteket

1. Lellky, Å. Katalog över orkester- och körverk, till-

144

gängliga för utlåning från Kungl. Musikaliska akademiens bibliotek och Sveriges orkesterföreningars riksförbunds centralbibliotek. 1953.

2. Johansson, C. French Music Publisher's Catalogues of the Second Half of the Eighteenth Century. 1955.

Quaderni dell'Accademia Musicale Chigiana
Siena: Libreria Ticci

1. Rudge, O. Lettere e dediche di Antonio Vivaldi. 1942.
2. Cecchini, G. La pacificazione fra Tolomei e Salimbeni. 1942.
3. Agosti, G. Osservazioni intorno alla tecnica pianistica. 1943.
4. Glinski, M. La prima stagione lirica italiana all'estero (1628). 1943.
5. Rinaldi, M. La data di nascita di Antonio Vivaldi. 1943.
6. Luin, E. J. Fortuna e influenza della musica di Pergolesi in Europa. 1943.
7. Cecchini, G. Le liti di confinazione fra Lucignano e Foiano. 1944.
8. Schena, G. Musica e religione. 1946.
9. Pignotti, G. Saena Civitas Virginis MCCLX-MCMXXXXVI. 1947.
10. Rinaldi, M. Il problema degli abbellimenti nell'Op. V di Corelli. 1947.
11. Salmi, M. Disegni di Francesco di Giorgio nella collezione Chigi Saracini. 1947.
12. Mario, E. A. Francesco Paolo Tosti (Conferenza tenuta nel Salone dell'Accademia Chigiana, il 16 Marzo 1947). 1947.
13. Rudge, O. Fac-simile di un autoggrafo di Antonio Vivaldi, con note sul Centro di Studi Vivaldiani all' Accademia Chigiana in Siena (1938-1947). 1947.
14. Raselli, A., & V. Mortari. In memoria dei Maestri dell'Accademia. Discorsi. 1947.
15. Bruers, A. Antonio Vivaldi; Fac-simile del Concerto

Funebre e discorso di A. Bruers per l'inaugurazione della V Settimana. Note e ricerche del Centro di Studi Vivaldiani. 1947.

16. Malherbe, Dom Benoit de. Alle prime fonti della musica; una teoria del ritmo musicale sulle basi del gregoriano. Riassunto delle conferenze. 1947.

17. Vannini, A., & R. de Rensis. In memoria di Ermanno Wolf-Ferrari. Contents: Incontro con il Maestro Ermanno Wolf-Ferrari, di A. Vannini; Conferenza di Raffaello de Rensis. 1948.

18. Corte, A. della. Baldassare Galuppi; profilo critico. 1948.

19. Cittadini, C. Tre canzoni di Guido Cavalcanti con i facsimili dei mss. senesi e la vita del poeta. 1949.

20. Rensis, R. de. Per Umberto Giordano e Ruggero Leoncavallo. 1949.

21. Borgatti, R. Osservazioni intorno al clavicembalo ben temperato di J.S. Bach. 1949.

22. Corte, A. della. Arrigo Serato (1877-1948). In appendice: Lettere di Busoni a Serato. 1950.

23. Schlitzer, F. Goethe e Cimarosa. Con un'appendice di note bio-bibliografiche. In occasione della VII Settimana Musicale (16-22 settembre 1950). 1950.

24. Bonaventura, A. Ricordi e ritratti. 1951.

25. Orsini, L., & E.A. Mario. Commemorazioni. Contents: Arrigo Boito, di L. Orsini; Francesco Cilèa, di E.A. Mario. 1951.

26. Schlitzer, F. Cimeli belliniani. 1952.

27. ----. Inediti verdiani nell'Archivio dell'Accademia Chigiana. 1953.

28. ----. L'ultima pagina della vita di Gaetano Donizetti; da un carteggio inedito dell'Accademia Chigiana. 1953.

29. Borgatti, R., & E. Pujol. Due aspetti del romanticismo. Contents: Schumann e Chopin, di Renata Borgatti; L'apporto italiano alla chitarra classica, di Emilio Pujol. 1953.

30. Schlitzer, F. L'eredità di Gaetano Donizetti, da carteggi e documenti dell'Archivio dell'Accademia Chigiana. 1954.

31. Cozzani, E. Per le Settimane Musicali Senesi; discorso inaugurale della X Settimana, 1953. 1954.

32. Luciani, S. A. Saggi e studi di Sebastiano A. Luciani, a cura di Giuseppe Caputi. Prefazione di Guido Chigi Saracini. 1954.

33. Schlitzer, F. Gaspare Spontini; frammenti biografici con lettere inedite. 1955.

34. ----. Antonio Sacchini; schede e appunti per una storia teatrale. 1955.

35. Rossini, G. Rossiniana; contributo all'epistolario di G. Rossini, a cura di Franco Schlitzer. 1956.

36. Raselli, A. L'Accademia Musicale Chigiana [1932-1956]; discorso commemorativo. 1956.

37. Schlitzer, F. Circostanze della vita di Gaspare Spontini con lettere inedite. 1958.

38. Chigi Saracini, G. , conte. Ricordanze; con note e illustrazioni, a cura di Olga Rudge. 1958.

39. Schlitzer, F. Rossini e Siena e altri scritti rossiniani (con lettere inedite). 1958.

40. Boito, A. Lettere inedite e poesie giovanili, a cura di Frank Walker. 1959.

41. Frazzi, V. I vari sistemi dell linguaggio musicale. 1960.

The Settimane Musicale of the Accademia Musicale Chigiana, which fall outside the scope of this study, are to be indexed in Vol. 20 of that series: Le celebrazioni del 1963. . ., con indice per autori e per materie dei voll. 1-20, a cura di Mario Fabbri, con la collaborazione di vari autori (in prep).

Quaderni di "Musica d'oggi"
Milano: Ricordi
  1. Scuola e musica. 1961. Scritti di vari giá pubbl. in

"Musica d'oggi," 1959-60. Premessa di R. Allorto.

Quaderni di "Vita nuova"
Parma: Scuola Tipografica Benedettina
1. Botti, F. Paganini e Parma; note storico-critiche di
   d. Ferruccio Botti. Prefazione di Pietro Berri. 1961.

Quellen und Forschungen zur musikalischen Folklore. Hrsg.
vom Institut für Musikforschung, Regensburg.
Regensburg: G. Bosse
1. Hoerburger, F. Katalog der europäischen Volksmusik
   im Schallarchiv des Instituts für Musikforschung Regensburg. 1952. (=Archives de la musique enregistrée,
   Série C, Vol. 4).
2. ----. Der Tanz mit der Trommel. 1954.
3. Au, H. von der. Deutsche Volkstänze aus der Dobrud-
   scha.

Quellenhefte zur Musikkunde und Musikgeschichte im Schul-
   unterricht
Dortmund: Crüwell
4. Moser, H. J., & O. Daube. Die Wittenbergisch Nachti-
   gall; Martin Luther und die Musik. 1962.

R. M. A. Research Chronicle
London: Royal Musical Association
1. Tilmouth, M. A Calendar of References to Music in
   Newspapers Published in London and the Provinces
   (1660-1719). 1961.
2. ----. Errata and General Index to [the above]. Also:
   Hugh Baillie, Some Biographical Notes on English Church
   Musicians, Chiefly Working in London (1485-1560).

Record Collector's Series
Hayes, Middlesex: E. M. I. Sales & Service
1. Demuth, N. Suggestions for Forming a Basic Library

148

of Gramaphone Records. 1949.
2. ----. Symphonies; Suggestions for a Representative
   Collection of Recordings, in Chronological Order, of
   Composers from Haydn to the Present day, With an Outline of Symphony Form. 1950.
3. ----. The Concerto. 1950.

Record Handbook
Stanhope, N. J. : Walter C. Allen
1. Mahony, D. The Columbia 13/14000-D Series; A
   Numerical Listing. 1961.

Régi magyar dallamok tára
Budapest: Akadémiai Kiadó
1. Csomasz Tóth, K. , ed. A XVI. század magyar dalla-
   mai. 1958.

Die Reihe; Information über serielle Musik. Hrsg. von
   Herbert Eimert unter Mitarbeit von Karlheinz
   Stockhausen.
Wien: Universal-Edition; Bryn Mawr, Penna. : Theodore
   Presser (English ed.)
1. Elektronische Musik. 1955. Electronic Music. 1958.
2. Anton Webern. 1955. Anton Webern. 1958.
3. Musikalisches Handwerk I. 1957. Musical Crafts-
   manship. 1959.
4. Junge Komponisten. 1958. Young Composers. 1960.
5. Berichte,   Analysen. 1959. Reports; Analyses. 1961.
6. Sprach und Musik. 1960. Speech and Music. 1964.
7. Form-Raum. 1960.
8. Rückblicke. 1962.

Royal School of Church Music. Study Notes.
Croyden, Surrey: Royal School of Church Music
1. Crook, H. Chanting for Beginners. 1957.
2. Saunders, P. Choir Training. 1957.

3. Crook, H. How to Form A Choir. 1957.
4. Pritchard, A. J. How to Train a Choir of Men and Women. 1958.
5. Routley, E. Hymn Tunes; An Historical Outline. 1959.
6. ----. Words of Hymns; A Short History. 1959.
7. Sumner, W. L. The Parish Church Organ. 1961.
8. Coleman, H. Conducting for Church Musicians. 1961.
9. Rainbow, B. How to Read Music. 1962.
10. Clarke, A. W. What Is Plainsong? 1964.
11. Fleming, M. P. M. The Accompaniment of Plainsong. 1964.

Saggi di storia e letteratura musicale. A cura di Giovanni da Nova.
Milano: Genio
1. Confalonieri, G. Prigionia di un artista; il romanzo di Luigi Cherubini. 2 vols. 1948.
2. Berlioz, H. Memorie, comprendenti i suoi viaggi in Italia, in Germania, in Russia, e in Inghilterra.
Versione italiana di Giulio e Maria Teresa Bas. 2 vols. 1947.
3. Landormy, P. C. R. Brahms. Versione italiana di Claudio Sartori. 1946.
4. Giazotto, R. Busoni; la vita nell'opera. 1947.

Sammlung musikwissenschaftlicher Einzeldarstellungen
Leipzig: Breitkopf und Härtel
1-17 before 1945.
18. Salmen, W. Das Lochamer Liederbuch; eine musikgeschichtliche Studie. 1951.

Sanssouci-Jazz-Bibliothek
Zürich: Sanssouci-Verlag
1. Morton, J. R. , & A. Lomax. Doctor Jazz Mister Jelly Rolls Moritat vom Jazz. Uebertragen von F. Herdi. 1960.

2. Bechet, S. Alle Kinder Gottes tragen eine Krone;
   eine Autobiographie. Uebertragen von F. Herdi. 1961.
3. Baker, D. Verklungene Trompete. Uebertragen von G.
   A. von Ihering und F. Herdi. 1961.
4. Goodman, B. Mein Weg zum Jazz; eine Autobiographie.
   Hrsg. und mit Zwischentexten versehen von I. Kolodin.
   Uebertragen von F. Herdi. 1961.

School of Bach-Playing for the Organist. Ed. by Gordon
   Phillips.
London: Hinrichsen
1. Phillips, G. Articulation in Organ Playing. Foreword
   by Robert Donington. 1961.
2. Sumner, W. L. Bach's Organ-Registration. Foreword
   by Ivor Keys. 1961.
3. Donington, R. Tempo and Rhythm in Bach's Organ
   Music. Foreword by Gordon Phillips. 1961.
4. Taylor, S. de B. Bach's Art of Part-Playing. 1964?

Schriften des Landesinstituts für Musikforschung, Kiel.
   [Vol. 14/: Kieler Schriften zur Musikwissenschaft]. Hrsg.
   von H. Albrecht.
Kassel: Bärenreiter
1. Brennecke, W. Die Handschrift A. R. 940/41 der
   Proske-Bibliothek zu Regensburg; ein Beitrag zur Musikgeschichte im zweiten Drittel des 16. Jahrhunderts.
   1953.
2. Schröder, I. M. Die Responsorienvertonungen des
   Balthasar Resinarius. 1954.
3. Hahne, G. Die Bach-Tradition in Schleswig-Holstein
   und Dänemark; eine musikhistorische Skizze. 1954.
4. Nausch, A. Augustin Pfleger, Leben und Werke; ein
   Beitrag zur Entwicklungsgeschichte der Kantate im 17.
   Jahrhundert. 1954 (i. e. 1955).
5. Ruhnke, M. Joachim Burmeister; ein Beitrag zur
   Musiklehre um 1600. 1955.

6. Weidemann, C. Leben und Wirken des Johann Philipp Förtsch, 1652-1732. 1955.

7. Mohr, P. Die Handschrift B 211-215 der Proske-Bibliothek zu Regensburg; mit kurzer Beschreibung der Handschriften B 216-219 und B 220-222. 1955.

8. Kölsch, H. Nicolaus Bruhns. 1958.

9. Schulz, J. A. P. , & J. H. Voss. Briefwechsel zwischen Johann Abraham Peter Schulz und Johann Heinrich Voss. 1960.

10. Riedel, F. W. Quellenkundliche Beiträge zur Geschichte der Musik für Tasteninstrumente in der zweiten Hälfte des 17. Jahrhunderts. 1960.

11. Detlefsen, H. P. Musikgeschichte der Stadt Flensburg bis zum Jahre 1850. 1961.

12. Schierning, L. Die Ueberlieferung der deutschen Orgel- und Klaviermusik aus der 1. Hälfte des 17. Jahrhunderts. 1961.

14. Hortschansky, K. Katalog der Kieler Musiksammlungen; die Notendrucke, Handschriften, Libretti und Bücher über Musik aus der Zeit bis 1830. 1963.

Schriftenreihe Das Musikinstrument
Frankfurt am Main: Verlag Das Musikinstrument

1. Pfeiffer, W. Ueber Dämpfer, Federn und Spielart. Neuauflage.

2. Herzog, H. K. Taschenbuch der Piano-Nummern deutscher und europäischer Instrumente; Klaviere, Flügel, Cembali, Harmonien. 1961.

3. Fenner, K. Die Berechnung der Spannung umsponnener Saiten; die Berechnung des Ueberganges von den umsponnenen Saiten zum Blankbezug. English ed. : On the Calculation of the Tension of Wound Strings; The Calculation of the Transition from Wound String to Wire. Supplement to: Fachbuchreihe Das Musikinstrument, Bd. 3. 1963.

4. Jung, K. Die physikalischen Grundlagen des Klavier-

baues; Akustik, Statik und Mechanik im Klavierbau.

5. Michel, J. Umgang mit Orgeln; kleine Schule des Registrierens und Wegweiser zu einer zeitgenössischen Orgel. 1963.

6. Ernst, F. Bach und das Pianoforte. 1963.

Schriftenreihe der Westfälischen Landeskirchenmusikschule in Herford.

Hrsg. von Wilhelm Ehmann.

Gütersloh: Rufer-Verlag

1. Ehmann, W. Erziehung zur Kirchenmusik. 1951.

2. Henche, H. Die gottesdienstliche Aufgabe der Kirchenmusik. 1951.

3. Honemeyer, K. Die Posaunenchöre im Gottesdienst. 1951.

4. Blankenburg, W. Kirchenlied und Volksliedweise. 1953.

5. Schönstedt, A. Alte westfälische Orgeln. 1953.

6. Voll, W. Die musikalische Neuordnung unseres Gottesdienstes. 1954.

No more appeared.

Schriftenreihe des Allgemeinen Cäcilien-Verbandes für die Länder der deutschen Sprache

Köln: Allgemeiner Cäcilien-Verband: No. 2: Wien; Herder

1. Musikalisches Brauchtum; Festschrift für Heinrich Lemacher. Hrsg. von seinen Freunden und Schülern. 1956.

2. Tittel, E. Oesterreichische Kirchenmusik; Werden, Wachsen, Wirken. 1961.

3. Overath, J., ed. Der Allgemeine Cäcilien-Verband für die Länder der deutschen Sprache; Gestalt und Aufgabe. 1961.

4. 4. Internationaler Kongress für Kirchenmusik in Köln 22.-30. Juni 1961; Dokumente und Berichte. Hrsg. von J. Overath. 1962.

5. Musicae sacrae ministerium; Beiträge zur Geschichte

der kirchenmusikalischen Erneuerung im 19. Jahrhundert.
Festgabe für Karl Gustav Fellerer zur Vollendung seines
60. Lebensjahres am 7. Juli 1962. Unter Mitarbeit
seiner Schüler und Freunde hrsg. von J. Overath. 1962.

Schriftenreihe des Schweizerischen Arbeitskreises für Kirchenmusik
Zürich: Zwingli-Verlag
2. Tappolet, W. In neuen Zungen; zur Frage des zeitgenössischen Kirchenliedes. 1963.

I Signori dell'armonia. Collezione di testi e studi musicali, diretta da L. Perrachio.
Torino: Edizione Palatine di R. Pezzani
1. Perrachio, L. Il clavicembalo ben temperato di G. S. Bach. 1947.
2. Pizzetti, I. La musica italiana dell'ottocento. 1947.

Solfèges
Paris: Éditions du Seuil
1. Citron, P. Couperin. 1956.
2. Boucourechliev, A. Schumann. 1956.
3. Jankélévitch, V. Ravel. 1956.
4. Schneider, M. Schubert. 1957.
5. Bourniquel, C. Chopin. 1957.
6. Barbaud, P. Haydn. 1957.
7. Landowski, M. Honegger. 1957.
8. Hocquard, J.-V. Mozart. 1958.
9. Francis, A. Jazz. 1958.
10. Petit, P. Verdi. 1958.
11. Hofmann, M. R. Tchaikovski. 1959.
12. Siohan, R. Stravinsky. 1959.
13. Campodonico, L. Falla. Trad. de Françoise Avila. 1959.
14. Roche, M. Monteverdi. 1960.
15. Rostand, C. Liszt. 1960.

16. Samuel, C. Prokofiev. 1960.
17. Schneider, M. Wagner. 1960.
18. Malignon, J. Rameau. 1960.
19. Marcel, L.-A. Bach. 1961.
20. Gauthier, A. Puccini. 1961.
21. Marnat, M. Moussorgsky. 1962.
22. Barraqué, J. Debussy. 1962.
23. Boucourechliev, A. Beethoven. 1963.
24. Citron, P. Bartók. 1963.

Sonatine-reeks. Onder redactie van Wouter Paap.
Tilburg: Nederland's Boekhuis
1. Nolthenius, H. Eroica; het leven van Ludwig van
   Beethoven. 1949.
2. Kortekaas, W. Het wonderkind van Salzburg; het leven
   van Wolfgang Amadeus Mozart. 1949.
3. Pool, R. E. Een handvol poolse aarde; het leven van
   Frédéric Chopin. 1950.
4. Uyldert, E. De cantor van de Thomaskerk; het
   leven van Johann Sebastian Bach. 1950.
5. Beke, C. De symphonie van het noodlot; het leven van
   Peter Iljitsj Tsjaikowski. 1950.
6. Kuin, J. P. W. De zanger van de italiaanse revolutie;
   het leven van Giuseppe Verdi. 1950.
7. Uyldert, E. Het eenzame hart; het leven van Robert
   Schumann. 1951.
8. Pool, R. E. Een nieuw lied voor Amerika; het leven
   van George Gershwin. 1951.
9. Schröder, A. E. De muzikant van Esterhazy; het leven
   van Jozef Haydn. 1951.
10. Nolthenius, H. Onvoltooide symphonie; het leven van
    Franz Schubert. 1952.
11. Kuin, J. P. W. Meteoor aan de operahemel; het leven
    van Gioachino Rossini. 1952.
12. Uyldert, E. Geen huis, geen vaderland; het leven van
    Johannes Brahms. 1953.
13. Elst, N. van der. Gelukskind; het leven van Felix

Mendelssohn Bartholdy. 1953.

14. ----. Organist van de Sinte Clotilde; het leven van
César Franck. 1953.

Spisy Janáčkovy akademie muzických umění
Prague: SPN

1. Vysloužil, J. Ludvík Kundera; monografie. 1962.

Srpska Akademija Nauka. Posebna Izdanja. Subseries:
Muzikološki Institut.

Beograd: Naucna Knjiga

1. Dordević, V. R. Prilozi biografskom recniku srpskih
muzicara. Posebna izdanja, Kniga 119. 1950.

2. Stankovič, Ž. Narodne pesme u krajini. Kniga
175. 1951.

3. Milankovič, B. Osnovi pijanističke umetnosti. Kniga 188.
1952.

4. Dragotin, C. Davor in jenko i njegovo doba. Kniga
201. 1952.

5. Vasiljevič, M. A. Narodne melodije iz Sandžaka. Kniga
205. 1953.

6. Manojlovič, K. P. Narodne melodije iz istočne Srbije.
Kniga 212. 1953.

7. Vučkovič, V. Izbor eseja. Urednik Stana Djurić-Klajn.
Kniga 233. 1955.

8. Milankovič, B.   Violina njena istorija i konstruk-
cija. Kniga 260. 1956.

9. Pašdan-Kojanov, S. Istoriski pazvoj gudačkih instrumen-
ata. Kniga 261. 1956.

10. Živkovič, M. Rukoveti st. st. mokranjca; analitička
studija. Kniga 283. 1957.

11. Vasiljevič, M. A. Narodne melodije leskovackog kraja.
Kniga 330. 1960.

Star-Galerie. Hrsg. von Karlheinz Hummel.

München: Neuzeit-Verlag

9. Conny. 1960.
10. Horst Buchholz. 1960.
11. Freddy Quinn. 1960.
12. Marion Michael. 1960.
13. Sabine Sinjen. 1960.
14. Peter Alexander. 1960.
15. O.W. Fischer. 1960.
16. Audrey Hepburn. 1960.
17. Christian Wolff. 1960.
18. Heidi Brühl. 1960.

Stimmen des XX. Jahrhunderts
Berlin: Max Hesses Verlag
1. Winckel, F. Klangwelt unter Lupe; aesthetisch-naturwissenschaftliche Betrachtungen, Hinweise zur Aufführungspraxis in Konzert und Rundfunk. 1952.
2. Rufer, J. Die Komposition mit zwölf Tönen. 1952.
3. Engel, H. Musik und Gesellschaft; Bausteine zu einer
Musiksoziologie. 1960.
4. Winckel, F. Phänomene des musikalischen Hörens;
aesthetisch-naturwissenschaftliche Betrachtungen,
Hinweise zur Aufführungspraxis in Konzert und Rundfunk.
1960.

Storia della musica
Milano: Fratelli Bocca
Serie 1
1. Borren, C. van den. Orlando di Lasso. 1944.
2. Ottani, G. Antonio Stradivari. 1945.
3. Valetta, I. Chopin; la vita e le opere. 1944. 7a ed.
1952.
4. Albertini, A. Beethoven; l'uomo. 4a ed. 1944. 5a ed.
1949.
5. Roncaglia, G. Rossini; l'olimpico. 1946. 2a ed. 1953.
6. Erb, J. L. Brahms; la vita e le opere. Trad.
di Pietro Leoni. 1946.

7. Lockspeiser, E. Debussy; la vita e le opere. Trad. di Pietro Leoni. 1946.

8. Coates, H. Palestrina; la vita e le opere. 1946.

9. Albertini, A. Mozart; la vita e le opere. 2a ed. 1946.

10. Roggeri, E. Schubert; la vita e le opere. 4a ed. 1946.

11. Elliot, J.H. Berlioz; la vita e le opere. 1947.

12. Einstein, A. Gluck; la vita e le opere. Trad. di Edoardo Roggeri. 1946.

13. Monaldi, G. Verdi; la vita e le opere. 3a ed. 1946. 5a ed. 1951.

14. D'Angeli, A. Benedetto Marcello; la vita e le opere. 1946.

15. Chamberlain, H.S. Wagner; la vita e le opere. 1947.

16. Albertini, A. Beethoven; epistolario. 2a ed. 1947.

17. Prunières, H. Lully; la vita e le opere. 1950.

Serie 2

1. Alaleona, D. Storia dell'oratorio musicale in Italia. 1945.

2. Giazotto, R. Tomaso Albinoni; musico di violino dilettante veneto (1671-1750). 1945. 2a ed. 1952.

3. Ghislanzoni, A. La storia della fuga. 1952.

4. Giazotto, R. Poesia melodrammatica e pensiero critico nel settecento. 1952.

5. Ghislanzoni, A. Luigi Rossi (Aloysius De Rubeis); biografia e analisi delle composizioni. 1954.

Pinzauti, L. La musica per liuto della prima metà del cinquecento. In prep.

Veggeti, A. Flauto e flautisti; storia e letteratura del flauto. In prep.

Studia i materiały do dziejów muzyki polskiej. Pod redakcją Tadeusza Strumiłły (1-4).
Kraków: PWM

1. Rudziński, W. Stanisław Moniuszko. Część 1, 1955. Część 2, 1961.

2. Prośnak, J. Kultura muzyczna Warszawy XVIII wieku. 1955. Dodatek muzyczny. 1956.
3. Strumiłło, T. Źródła i początki romantyzmu w muzyce polskiej; studia i materiały. Dodatek nutowy. 1956.
4. Nowak-Romanowicz, A. Józef Elsner. 1957.
5. Poźniak, W. Eugeniusz Pankiewicz. 1958.
6. Wroński, W. Zygmunt Noskowski. 1960.

Studia musicologica upsaliensia. Edidit Carl-Allan Moberg. Uppsala: Almqvist & Wiksell
1. Davidsson, Å. Catalogue critique et descriptif des imprimés de musique des XVIe et XVIIe siècles conservés dans les bibliothèques suédoises (excepté la Bibliothèque de l'Université Royale d'Upsala). 1952.
2. ----. Catalogue critique et descriptif des ouvrages théoriques sur la musique imprimés au XVIe et au XVIIe siècles et conservés dans les bibliothèques suédoises. 1953.
3. Bengtsson, I., & R. Danielson. Handstilar och not-pikturer i Kungl. Musikaliska akademiens Roman-samling. 1955.
4. ----. J.H. Roman och hans instrumentalmusik; käll- och stilkritiska studier. With an English summary. 1955.
5. Davidsson, Å. Studier rörande svenskt musiktryck före år 1750. 1957.
6. Hambraeus, B. Codex carminum gallicorum; une étude sur le volume Musique vocale du manuscrit 87 de la Bibliothèque de l'Université d'Upsala. 1961.
7. Davidsson, Å. Danskt musiktryck intill 1700-talets mitt. 1962.

Studienmaterial für die künstlerischen Lehranstalten der Deutschen Demokratischen Republik. Reihe: Musik. Hrsg. vom Ministerium für Kultur, Hauptabteilung künstlerische Lehranstalten.
Dresden: Verlag der Kunst; Berlin: Ministerium für Kultur,

Hauptabteilung künsterlische Lehranstalten (1955, H. 2-)

1954, Heft. 1. Meissner, H. Die jugendliche Stimme und ihre pflegliche Behandlung.

2. Aspelund, D. Die Entwicklung des Sängers und seiner Stimme. Hrsg. von M. Lwow, Musgis, 1952. Uebers. und ausgew. von E. M. Arndt.

3. Richard Wagner. Contents: (1) W. Konen, "Richard Wagner" Aus: Presse der SU, Nr. 130, 1953; (2) Hans Mayer, "Richard Wagners geistige Entwicklung." Aus: Sinn und Form, Heft 3/4, 1953.

4. Smetana-Janáček. Contents: (1) Vladimír Helfert, "Die schöpferische Entwicklung Friedrich Smetanas"; (2) J. Racek und C. Hálová-Jahodová, "Leoš Janáček; Leben und Werk." Aus: Leoš Janáček; Leben und Werk (Pokorny: Brünn, 1948). Aus dem Tschechischen übers. von Bruno Liehm.

5. Schulze, H. Zur Frage der ästhetischen Anschauungen Robert Schumanns.

1955, Heft 1. Jiránek, J. Volkschina in der Musik. Aus "Hudební rozhledy" VII (9)/1954. Aus dem Tschechischen übers. von Bruno Liehm.

2. Musik der französischen bürgerlichen Revolution. Uebers. von H. Schulze und H. Krüger.

3 and 4, 1955, did not appear.

1956, Heft 1. Worbs, H. C. Die Sinfonik Haydns.

2. Alekseev, A. D. Geschichte der Klaviermusik und ihrer Interpretation. Uebers. von Karl Krämer; gekürzt und bearbeitet von Karl Schinsky.

3. Margenburg, E. Carl Maria von Weber in Briefen und Schriften; Auswahl und Kommentar.

4. Goldschmidt, H., G. Knepler, & E. H. Meyer. Musik-geschichte im Ueberblick. Teil 1: Von der Urgesellschaft bis zur Renaissance.

Summa musicae medii aevi. Hrsg. von Friedrich Gennrich. Darmstadt: F. Gennrich

1. Guillaume de Machaut. La messe de Nostre-Dame. Faksimile-Ausgabe, hrsg. von F. Gennrich. 1957.
2. Gennrich, F. Bibliographie der ältesten französischen und lateinischen Motetten. 1957.
3-4. ----. Der musikalische Nachlass der Troubadours. Bd. 1: Kritische Ausgabe der Melodien. 1958. Bd. 2: Kommentar. 1960.
5. ----. Die Wimpfener Fragmente der Hessischen Landesbibliothek, Darmstadt. Faksimile-Ausgabe der Handschrift 3471. 1958.
6. ----. Ein altfranzösischer Motettenkodex. Faksimile-Ausgabe der Handschrift La Clayette, Paris Bibl. Nat. nouv. acq. fr. 13521. 1958.
7-8. Ludwig, F. Repertorium organorum recentioris et motetorum vetustissimi stili. Bd. I/2: Handschriften in Mensuralnotation; die Quellen der Motetten ältesten Stils. Bd. II: Musikalisches Anfangs-Verzeichnis des nach Tenores geordneten Repertorium. Hrsg. von F. Gennrich.
9. Neidhart von Reuenthal. Neidhart-Lieder. Kritische Ausgabe der Neidhart von Reuenthal zugeschriebenen Melodien, hrsg. von F. Gennrich. 1962.
10. Gennrich, F. Das altfranzösische Rondeau und Virelai im 12. und 13. Jahrhundert. In prep.
11. ----. Die Jenaer Liederhandschrift. Faksimile-Ausgabe ihrer Melodien. 1963.

Summy Piano Teaching Pamphlet Series
Chicago: Summy Publishing Company

7. Ilg, F. L. , & L. B. Ames. Child Behavior. 1956.
8. Newman, W. S. Styles and Touches in Bach's Keyboard Music. 1956.
9. Dumesnil, M. Pedaling. 1956.
10. Newman, W. S. Styles and Touches in Mozart's Keyboard Music. 1956.
11. Dumesnil, M. Interpreting Debussy. 1957.

12. Cazedessus, D. Contemporary Sounds in Piano Teaching Literature. 1957.

Several of these papers, together with
some others, are bound together in Handbook for Piano Teachers; Collected Articles on Subjects Related to Piano Teaching (Evanston, Ill.: Summy-Birchard Publishing Company, 1958).

Symposium. Collana di studi musicali diretta da Guido M. Gatti.
Milano: Ricordi
1. Amico, F. d', & G. M. Gatti. Alfredo Casella.
   Con saggi di Dante Alderighi et al. 1958.
2. Sartori, C. Giacomo Puccini. Con saggi di Paul Acker et al. 1959.
3. Mila, M. Manuel de Falla. Con saggi di Melchior de Almagro San Martin et al e scritti di Manuel de Falla. Trad. di Mario Bortolotto et al. 1962.

Tübinger Bach-Studien. Hrsg. von Walter Gerstenberg.
Trossingen/Württemberg: Math. Hohner
1. Dadelsen, G. von. Bemerkungen zur Handschrift J. S. Bachs, seiner Familie und seines Kreises. 1957.
2/3. Kast, P. Die Bach-Handschriften der Berliner Staatsbibliothek. 1958.
4/5. Dadelsen, G. von. Beiträge zur Chronologie der Werke Johann Sebastian Bachs. 1958.

Universidad de Chile, Instituto de Investigaciones Musicales, Facultad de Ciencias y Artes Musicales. Colección de ensayos.
Santiago de Chile: Imprenta Universitaria
1. Pereira Salas, E. La música de la Isal de Pascua. 1947?
2. Vega, C. La forma de la cueca chilena. 194-.
3. Orrego Salas, J. Aarón Copland; un músico de Nueva

York. 194-.
4. Mendoza, V. T. La canción chilena en México. 1948.
5. Lavín, C. N. S. de las Peñas; ritual del norte de Chile. 194-.
6. García Morillo, R. Julián Bautista en la música española contemporánea. 194-.
7. Salas Viu, V. Chopin y las dos caras del romanticismo. 1949.
8. Lavín, C. La Tirana; fiesta ritual del norte de Chile. 195-.

   Hornbostel, E. M. von. La música de los Fueguinos y Patagones.

University of California Publications in Music. Ed. by G. S. McManus & W. H. Rubsamen et al.
Berkeley & Los Angeles: University of California Press
1, no. 1. Rubsamen, W. H. Literary Sources of Secular Music in Italy (ca. 1500). 1943.
1, no. 2. Tusler, R. L. The Style of J. S. Bach's Chorale Preludes. 1956.
2, no. 1. Poladian, S. S. Armenian Folk-Songs. 1942.
2, no. 2. Bukofzer, M. F. "Sumer is icumen in"; A Revision. 1944.
3. Nelson, R. U. The Technique of Variation. 1948.
4. Vincent, J. N. The Diatonic Modes in Modern music. 1951.
5. Marrocco, W. T. The Music of Jacopo da Bologna. 1954.
6. May, E. The influence of the Meiji Period on Japanese Children's Music. 1963.

Utrechtse bijdragen tot de muziekwetenschap. Uitgegeven vanwege het Instituut voor Muziekwetenschap der Rijksuniversiteit te Utrecht onder leiding van Prof. Dr. Eduard Reeser.
Bilthoven: A. B. Creyghton

1. Tusler, R. L. The Organ Music of Jan Pieterszoon Sweelinck. 2 vols. 1958.
2. Meer, J. H. van der. Johann Josef Fux als Opernkomponist. 4 Bände in 3. 1961.
3. Gleich, C. von. Die Sinfonischen Werke von Alexander Skrjabin. 2 Bände. 1963.

Veröffentlichungen der Gesellschaft der Orgelfreunde. Hrsg. von Walter Supper.

Berlin: Merseburger (1-7, 9, 11-15, 22); Kassel: Bärenreiter (8, 21); Cuxhaven: Oliva-Verlag (10, 16); München: Verlag Georg D. W. Callwey (17); Zürich: Zwingli-Verlag (20). Partly music.

1. Supper, W., ed. Der Barock, seine Orgeln und seine Musik in Oberschwaben; zugleich der Bericht über die Tagung in Ochsenhausen 1951. 1952.
2. ----. Alte Orgelmusik (Bach-Strebel, Melchior, Schildt). 1952. 3. Auflage 1960.
3. Siegele, U., ed. Musik des Oberschwäbischen Barock. 1952.
4. Supper, W., ed. Neue Orgelmusik (Bonitz-Rövenstrunck). 1952. 3. Auflage 1963.
5. Klotz, H., & W. Supper, ed. Orgelgehäusezeichnungen von A. G. Hill (Jahresgabe 1952). 1953.
6. Quoika, R., ed. Altbayern als Orgel-Landschaft; zugleich der Bericht über das 1. Orgeltreffen der Gesellschaft der Orgelfreunde in Ingolstadt-Weltenburg vom 3. bis 5. Oktober 1953. 1954.
7. ----. Albert Schweitzers Begegnung mit der Orgel. 1954.
8. Supper, W. Der sparsame Orgelsachberater (Neujahrsgabe 1956).
9. Adelung, W. Elektronen-Instrument und Pfeifen-Orgel (Jahresgabe 1956). 1956.
10. Seggermann, G., ed. Klingende Schätze; Orgelland zwischen Weser und Elbe (Jahresgabe 1957).

11. Quoika, R. Altbayerische Orgeltage (Tagungsbericht über das Freisinger Orgeltreffen 1956; Grosse Jahresgabe 1956). 1958.
12. Supper, W., ed. Richtlinien zum Schutze alter wertvoller Orgeln (Weilheimer Regulativ). 1958.
13. Summaria der ergetzlichen Begebenheytten des Orgelmachers Daniel Brustwerckle. In prep.
14. Supper, W., ed. Orgelbewegung und Historismus (Jahresgabe 1954 und 1955). 1958.
15. Quoika, R. Altösterreichische Hornwerke; ein Beitrag zur Frühgeschichte der Orgelbaukunst. 1959.
16. Rihsé, V. & G. Seggermann. Klingendes Friesland. 1959.
17. Supper, W. Kleines Orgelbrevier für Architekten (Jahresgabe 1958).
18. Bunk, G. Liebe zur Orgel; Erinnerungen aus einem Musikleben. 2. Auflage 1958.
19. Kern, E. Die Orgel (Sonderdruck als Jahresgabe 1960).
20. Knoepfli, A. Von der schweizerischen Orgeldenkmalpflege (Jahresgabe 1959).
21. Die Orgel in Geschichte und Gegenwart. Festgabe zum zehnjährigen Bestehen der Gesellschaft der Orgelfreunde (Jahresgabe 1961).
22. Das Elektrium; Beitrag zur Klärung der Frage Orgel--Orgelimitation. Von W. Adelung [et al]. 1964.

Veröffentlichungen der Hamburger Telemann-Gesellschaft
Hamburg: H. Sikorski
1. Valentin, E. Telemann in seiner Zeit; Versuch eines geistesgeschichtlichen Porträts. 1960.
2. Barthe, E. Takt und Tempo; Studien über die Zusammenhänge von Takt und Tempo. Vorwort von Karl Grebe. 1960.

Veröffentlichungen der Kommission für Musikforschung.
Subseries of: Sitzungsberichte der phil.-hist. Klasse der

Oesterreichischen Akademie der Wissenschaften.

Graz, Wien, Köln: H. Böhlau

1. Schenk, E. Ein unbekannter Brief Leopold Mozarts. Mit Beiträge zum Leben und Werk W. A. Mozarts. 1947.
2. Weinmann, A. Wiener Musikverleger und Musikalien-händler von Mozarts Zeit bis gegen 1860; ein firmen-geschichtlicher und topographischer Behelf. Festgabe der Akademie für die Teilnehmer des Internationalen Musik-wissenschaftlichen Kongresses Wien, Mozartjahr 1956. 1956. Wien: Rohrer in Kommission.
3. Wessely-Kropik, H. Lilio Colista, ein römischer Meister vor Corelli; Leben und Umwelt. 1961.

Veröffentlichungen des Beethovenhauses in Bonn. Neue Folge. Im Auftrag des Vorstandes hrsg. von Prof. Dr. Joseph Schmidt-Görg.

Bonn: Beethovenhaus (Vierte Reihe: München-Duisburg: G. Henle)

1. Reihe. Beethoven; Skizzen und Entwürfe.
2. Reihe. Beethoven-Jahrbuch.
3. Reihe. Beethoven; Ausgewählte Handschriften in Fak-simile-Ausgabe.

Series 1-3 are outside the scope of this study.

4. Reihe. Schriften zur Beethovenforschung.

1. Schmidt-Görg, J. Beethoven; die Geschichte seiner Familie. In prep.
2. Mies, P. Textkritische Untersuchungen bei Beethoven. 1957.
3. Misch, L. Die Faktoren der Einheit in der Mehrsätzig-keit der Werke Beethovens; Versuch einer Theorie der Einheit des Werkstils. 1958.

Veröffentlichungen des Instituts für neue Musik und Musik-erziehung Darmstadt

Berlin: Merseburger

1. Stilkriterien der neuen Musik; fünf Beiträge von Sieg-

fried Borris, Hans Heinz Dräger, Wilhelm Keller, Walter
Kolneder und Fritz Winckel. 1961.

2. Stilporträts der neuen Musik; sieben Beiträge von Siegfried Borris, Wilhelm Keller, Heinrich Lindlar, Walter
Kolneder und Winfried Zillig. 1961.

3. Der Wandel des musikalischen Hörens; neun Beiträge
von Siegfried Borris, Karl Gustav Fellerer, Günter
Hausswald, Hermann Heiss, Walter Kolneder, Joseph
Müller-Blattau, Hermann Pfrogner, Hans-Peter Reinecke
und Rudolf Stephan. 1962.

4. Vergleichende Interpretationskunde; sieben Beiträge von
S. Borris, A. Feil, S. Goslich, W. Kolneder, W.-E. von
Lewinski, H. Lindlar und J. Müller-Blattau. 1963.

Veröffentlichungen des Max-Reger-Institutes, Elsa-Reger-
Stiftung, Bonn

Bonn: Ferd. Dümmler

1. Max Regers 75. Geburstag; Zwei Reden. Contents: J.
Haas, "Max Reger," & H. Mersmann, "Reger und seine
Zeit." 1948.

2. Festschrift für Elsa Reger anlässlich ihres 80.
Geburtstages am 25. Oktober 1950. Erinnerungen und
Beiträge persönlicher Reger-Freunde. 1950.

3. Reger, M. Briefe zwischen der Arbeit; als Erstveröf-
fentlichung im Auftrage des Kuratoriums des Max-
Reger-Institutes hrsg. von Ottmar Schreiber. 1956.

Voices of the Past; A Catalogue of Vocal Recordings
Tandridge Lane, Lingfield, Surrey: The Oakwood Press

1. Bennett, J.R. A Catalogue of Vocal Recordings from
the English Catalogues of The Gramophone Company 1898-
1899, The Gramophone Company Limited 1899-1900; The
Gramophone & Typewriter Company Limited 1901-1907,
and The Gramophone Company Limited 1907-1925. Cover
title: Vocal Recordings 1898-1925; Volume 1: The Gramophone Company Limited (HMV); English Catalogue. 1957?

2. Bennett, J. R. A Catalogue of Vocal Recordings from The Italian Catalogues of The Gramophone Company Limited 1899-1900, The Gramophone Company (Italy) Limited 1899-1909, The Gramophone Company Limited 1909, Compagnia Italiana del Grammofono 1909-1912, & Società Nazionale del Grammofono 1912-1925.
Cover title: Vocal Recordings 1898-1925; Volume 2: The Gramophone Company Limited (HMV); Italian Catalogue.
3. [Fonotipia Supplement].
4. Bennett, J. R., & E. Hughes. The International Red Label Catalogue of "DB" & "DA"; His Master's Voice Recordings 1924-1956. Book 1: "DB" (12 inch).
5. Smith, M. The Catalogue of "D" & "E"; His Master's Voice Recordings. 1961.

Wiener Abhandlungen zur Musikwissenschaft und Instrumentenkunde. Hrsg. von Hugo Alker.
Wien: Geyer
1. Alker, H. Die Blockflöte; Instrumentenkunde, Geschichte, Musizierpraxis. 1962.
2. ----. Literatur für alte Tasteninstrumente; Versuch einer Bibliographie für die Praxis. 1962.
3. Dawidowicz, A. Orgelbaumeister und Orgeln in Ost-Tirol.
4. Pantscheff, E. Die Entwicklung der Oper in Bulgarien von ihren Anfängen bis 1915. 1962.
5. Langer, A. Das Problem des Geigenbaues.
6. Haupt, H. Wiener Instrumentenbau um 1800.
Grasberger, F. Musikbibliographie.
Benedikt, E. Zur Aufführungspraxis der alten Musik.

Wiener Musik-Bücherei
Wien: Ludwig Doblinger
3. Liess, A. Wiener Barockmusik. 1946.
Apparently no others appeared.

Wiener musikwissenschaftliche Beiträge. Unter Leitung von
  Erich Schenk.
Graz, Köln, Wien: H. Böhlau
  1. Eberstaller, O. Orgeln und Orgelbauer in Oesterreich.
     1955.
  2. Bauer, A. Opern und Operetten in Wien; Verzeichnis
     ihrer Erstaufführungen in der Zeit von 1629 bis zur
     Gegenwart. 1955.
  3. Hertel, J.W. Autobiographie; hrsg. und kommentiert
     von Erich Schenk. 1957.
  4. Wessely, O. Arnold von Bruck und die Wiener Hofkapel-
     le von 1519 vis 1545. In prep.
  5. Gericke, H. Der Wiener Musikalienhandel von 1700 bis
     1778. 1960.

Wir fangen an
Leipzig: Hofmeister
  1. Bimberg, S. Wie leite ich ein offenes Singen? 1956.
  2. Donath, P. Tonsatzlehre. Teil 1. 1958.
  3. Bimberg, S. Wie gestalte ich ein Programm? Die
     Programmgestaltung als Grundlage inhaltlicher Aussage.
     1957.
  4. ----. Musikpädagogische Grundlagen der Chorerziehung.
     1957.
  5. Lange, C. Wege zur wirkungsvollen Liedgestaltung;
     eine Anleitung für Singegruppen und ihre Leiter. 1959.
  6. Bimberg, S. , & F. Bachmann. Musizieren mit klingen-
     dem Schlagwerk; rhythmische und melodische Erziehung
     im Gruppenunterricht. 1958.

The World of Music. Ed. by Sir George Franckenstein and
  Otto Erich Deutsch.
London: Parrish; N.Y.: Chanticleer Press
  1. Herbage, J. Messiah. 1948.
  2. Gál, H. The Golden Age of Vienna. 1948.
  3. King, A.H. Chamber Music. 1948.

4. Shawe-Taylor, D. Covent Garden. 1948.
5. Carner, M. The Waltz. 1948.
6. Schumann, E. German Song. 1948.
7. Cooper, M. Opéra comique. 1949.
8. Carse, A. von Ahn. The Orchestra. 1949.
9. Russell, T. A. The Proms. 1949.
10. Culshaw, J. The Concerto. 1949.
11. Robertson, A. Sacred Music. 1950.
12. Farmer, H. G. Military Music. 1950.
13. Jacobs, A. Gilbert and Sullivan. 1951.
14. Cooper, M. Russian Opera. 1951.
15. Toye, J. F. Italian Opera. 1952.

London series numbered; U. S. unnumbered

Yale Studies in the History of Music. Ed. by Leo Schrade.
New Haven, Conn.: Yale University Press
1. Cannon, B. C. Johann Mattheson; Spectator in Music.
   1947.
2. Waite, W. G. The Rhythm of Twelfth-Century Polyphony; Its Theory and Practice. 1954.
3. Knapp, J. The Polyphonic Conductus of the Notre-
   Dame Epoch. To be pub. in 1964.

Young Reader's Guide to Music
London: Oxford University Press
1. Gough, C. Boyhoods of Great Composers. 1960.
2. Hosier, J. The Sorcerer's Apprentice, and Other
   Stories. 1960.
3. Appleby, W. & F. Fowler. Nutcracker and
   Swan Lake. 1960.
4. Bruxner, M. The Orchestra. 1960.
5. Crozier, E. Let's Make an Opera. 1962.
6. Gough, C. Boyhoods of Great Composers. Book 2.
   1963.
7. Crozier, E. The Mastersingers of Nuremberg. 1963.
8. -----. The Magic Flute; Letters from Mozart to His

Sister. 1963.

Za novou hudbu
Praha: Orbis
3. Sychra, A. Stranická hudební kritika-spolutvůrce nové
hudby; úvod do hudební estetiky socialistického realismu.
1951.
4. Nestěv, I., & J. Kremlev. O realismu v hudbě.
Přel. I. Vojtěch. 1952.
6. Jiránek, J. Zdeněk Nejedlý, učitel mladé generace.
1952.
7. Sychra, A. O hudbu zítřka; soubor studií a článků.
1952.

Zenetudományi tanulmányok. Szerk. Szabolcsi Bence és
Bartha Dénes.
Budapest: Akadémiai Kiadó
1. Szabolcsi, B. & D. Bartha, ed. Emlékkönyv Kodály
Zoltán 70. születésnapjára. 1953.
2. ----. Erkel Ferenc és Bartók Béla emlékére. 1954.
3. ----. Liszt Ferenc és Bartók Béla emlékére. 1955.
4. ----. A magyar zene történetéből. 1955.
5. ----. W. A. Mozart emlékére. 1957.
6. ----. Zenetudományi tanulmányok Kodály Zoltán 75.
születésnapjára. 1957.
7. ----. Bartók Béla megjelenése az európai zeneéletben
(1914-1926). Liszt Ferenc hagyatéka. 1959.
8. ----. Zenetudományi tanulmányok Haydn emlékére.
1960.
9. ----. Az opera történetéből. 1961.
10. ----. Bartók Béla emlékére. 1962.

Zródła pamiętnikarsko-literackie do dziejów muzyki
polskiej. Red. Tadeusz Strumiłło (1-6).
Kraków: PWM
1. Kurpiński, K. Dziennik podróży 1823. Opracował Z.

Jachimecki. Wyd. 2. 1957.

2. Ogiński, M. K. Listy o muzyce. Opracował Tadeusz Strumiłło. 1956.

3. Każyński, W. Notatki z podróży muzykalnej po Niemczech odbytej w roku 1844. Opracował W. Rudziński. 1957.

4. Elsner, J. Sumariusz moich utworów muzycznych. Red. Alina Nowak-Romanowicz. 1957.

5. Szymanowski, K. Z listów. Opracowała Teresa Bronowicz-Chylińska. 1958.

6. ----. Z pism. Opracowała Teresa Bronowicz-Chylińska. 1958.

7. Chybiński, A. W czasach Straussa i Tetmajera; wspomnienia. Opracowali Anna i Zygmunt Szweykowscy. 1958.

8. Anders, H. Mieczysław Karłowicz w listach i wspomnieniach. 1960.

9. Paderewski, I. J. Pamiętniki. Spisała Mary Lawton. Przeł. Wanda Lisowska i Teresa Mogilnicka. Wstęp: Witold Rudziński. 1961.

10. Świerzewski, S. J. I. Kraszewski i polskie życie muzyczne XIX wieku. 1963.

172

Index of Names

A

Aaengenvoort, Johannes, 100
Abbiati, Franco, 82
Abert, Hermann, 49
Abraham, Gerald, 36
Abraham, Lars Ulrich, 47
Absil, Jean, 56
Acker, Paul, 162
Ackere, Jules van, 102, 142
Adam de la Halle, 127
Adelung, Wolfgang, 164, 165
Adlung, Jakob, 72, 73
Adrian, P. G., 73
Adrio, Adam, 47
Agosti, Guido, 145
Alain, Olivier, 55
Alaleona, Domenico, 158
Albersheim, Gerhard, 62
Albertini, Alberta, 157, 158
Albinoni, Tomaso, 158
Albrecht, Hans, 72, 125, 151
Albrecht, Julius, 74
Alcini, I., 50
Aldefeld, A., 96
Alderighi, Dante, 162
Aldrich, Putnam, 37
Alekseev, A. D., 160
Alexander, Peter, 157
Alf, J., 42, 43
Alker, Hugo, 168
Allaire, Gaston, 116
Allegri, Gregorio, 78
Allen, Walter C., 91
Allorto, Lily, 141
Allorto, Riccardo, 86, 141, 148
Almagro San Martin, Melchior de, 162
Alpaerts, Flor, 56
Altmann, Wilhelm, 82
Amann, Julius, 78
Ames, Louise Bates, 161
Amico, Fedele d', 162
Amis, John, 71

Ancina, Giovanni Giovenale, 65
Anders, Henryk, 172
Anderson, Hugh, 54
Anderson, L., 90
Anderson, W. R., 84
Andreae, Volkmar, 129
Angeli, Andrea d', 158
Angelini-Bontempi, Giovanni Andrea, 86
Anglès, Higinio (Higini), 69
Anonymous, 58, 69, 70
Anonymous IV, 111
Anschuez (Anschütz), Joseph Andreas, 44
Anselmo, Giorgio, 86
Anson, Hugo Vernon, 130
Antcliffe, Herbert, 85
Antes, John, 109
Apel, Willi, 62
Appleby, William, 170
Araiz Martínez, Andrés, 60
Arakélian, Sourène, 75
Argine, Costantino dall', 113
Aribo Scholasticus, 69
Armstrong, Louis, 91, 93, 96, 104
Armstrong, Thomas, 58
Arndt, E. M., 121, 160
Arnold, John Henry, 57, 58
Artaria, publisher, 41
Aschoff, Volker, 42
Aspelund, Dmitriĭ, 160
Au, Hans von der, 148
Augustinus, Aurelius (St. Augustine), 62
Avila, Françoise, 154
Ayestarán, Lauro, 110

173

Fučiková, Jitka, 95
Funke, Otto, 75, 76
Furlotti, Arnaldo, 113
Fux, Johann Josef, 164

G

Gabrieli, Giovanni, 110, 116
Gabryś, Jerzy, 105
Gaeta. See Mario.
Gaillard, André, 72
Gajard, Joseph, 50
Gál, Hans, 169
Galilei, Vincenzo, 115
Gall, Hannes, 140
Gallico, Claudio, 86
Galpin, Francis William, 63
Galuppi, Baldassare, 146
Gamberini, Leopoldo, 86
García Morillo, Roberto, 163
Gardavský, Čeněk, 70
Gardener, G., 58
Gardien, Jacques, 64
Gasparini, Francesco, 111
Gastinois, Ernoul de, 116
Gastoué, Amédée, 143
Gatti, Guido Maria, 162
Gauthier, André, 155
Gavazzeni, Gianandrea, 81, 82, 111
Gavoty, Bernard, 55, 80, 81
Geehl, Henry, 85
Geering, Arnold, 143
Gehrels, Willem, 128
Gelineau, Joseph, 93
Gennrich, Friedrich, 102, 126, 160, 161
George, Stefan, 35
Georgiades, Thrasybulos, 107, 109
Geraedts, Henri, 68, 79
Geraedts, Jaap, 68, 79
Gerbert, Martin, 61
Gerhardt, Carl, 124
Gericke, Hannelore, 169
Gershwin, George, 51, 68, 83, 106, 112, 155
Gerstenberg, Walter, 162
Gerth, Joachim, 91
Gessner, Erika, 47
Ghislanzoni, Alberto, 158
Gianturco, Elio, 107

Giazotto, Remo, 150, 158
Gide, André, 120
Giegling, Franz, 129
Gilbert, Will G., 127, 128
Gilbert, Sir William Schwenck, 170
Gilles, André, 70
Gillespie, Dizzy, 90, 91, 93
Gilson, Paul, 102
Giordano, Umberto, 146
Giorgio, Francesco di, 145
Giustiniani, Vicenzo, 115
Glareanus, Henricus, 115
Glass, Louis, 120
Glauch. See Becker-Glauch.
Gleich, C. von, 164
Gletle, Johann Melchior, 143
Glinka, Mikhail Ivanovich, 121
Glinski, Matteo (Mateusz), 145
Gluck, Christoph Willibald, 96, 122, 123, 140, 158
Göller, Gottfried, 100
Göllerich, August, 127
Göllner, Theodor, 110
Goes, Damião de, 35
Goethe, Johann Wolfgang von, 96, 103, 129, 146
Götze, Werner, 91
Gokita, H., 102
Golachowski, Stanisław, 53
Goldman, Richard Franko, 77
Goldschmidt, Harry, 160
Goléa, Antoine, 55
Gołowiński, G., 104
Goodman, Benjamin David "Benny," 91, 151
Gorodinski, W. (V. Gorodinskii), 118
Goslich, S., 167
Gossec, François-Joseph, 64
Gottron, Adam, 41
Gough, Catherine, 170
Goya y Lucientes, Francisco Jose de, 52
Graaf, M. E. de, 136
Grabner, Hermann, 82, 83
Grace, Harvey, 58
Gram, Peder, 120
Grasberger, Franz, 123,

189

104, 105, 121
Rinaldi, Mario, 81, 82, 145
Ring, Oluf, 120
Ringbom, Nils-Eric, 102, 122
Risinger, Karel, 88, 89, 98
Rivière, M.-A., 93, 94
Robert, Walter, 115
Robert de Handlo, 111
Roberts, Robert Edwin, 58
Robertson, Alec, 85, 170
Robijns, J., 56
Robson, W.A., 85
Roche, Maurice, 154
Rödig, Hans, 76
Röntgen, Julius, 49
Roger, Estienne, 57
Roggeri, Edoardo, 158
Rognoni, Luigi, 51
Rohlfs, Eckart, 78
Roland-Manuel (Roland Alexis Manuel Lévy), 55, 80, 141
Rolland, Romain, 74, 94, 97, 105
Rollin, Jean, 143
Roman, Johan H., 159
Romanowicz. See Nowak-Romanowicz.
Roncaglia, Gino, 51, 81, 86, 157
Ronga, Luigi, 107
Ronsard, Pierre de, 143
Rosanti, Cara, 107
Rosenmüller, Johann, 61
Rosenwald, Hans, 106
Rosier, Carl, 44
Rossi, Luigi, 158
Rossini, Gioacchino, 51, 67, 79, 82, 88, 92, 94, 104, 113, 147, 155, 157,
Rostand, Claude, 64, 107, 154
Roth, Joachim, 100
Rothärmel, Marion, 101
Roussel, Albert, 64, 65, 80, 81
Routley, Erik, 150
Rouvel, Diether, 100
Różycki, Ludomir, 53
Rubsamen, Walter Howard, 163
Rucker, Arnold, 41
Rudge, Olga, 145, 147

Rudolf, Haupt, 38
Rudziński, Witold, 104, 105, 158, 172
Rufer, Josef, 157
Ruhnke, Martin, 72, 151
Rusconi, Gerardo, 51
Russell, Thomas Alfred, 170
Rust, Brian A.L., 91
Rutgerus Sycamber de Venray, 46
Rutters, Herman, 68, 79
Rychlík, Jan, 70, 89

S

Saam, Joseph, 61
Sacchini, Antonio, 147
Sachs, Curt, 59, 123
Sádecký, Zdeněk, 97
Saint-Saëns, Camille, 65
Salas Viu, Vicente, 137, 163
Salimbeni family, 145
Salinas, Francisco de, 72
Salmen, Walter, 117, 150
Salmi, Mario, 145
Salomon, A., 83
Sambeth, Heinrich M., 39
Sambucetti, Luis, 110
Sampayo Ribeiro, Mário de, 35
Samson, Joseph, 142
Samuel, C., 155
Sand, George, pseud. (Mme. Dudevant), 52
Sanders, Paul F., 49
Santen, Rient van, 48
Saracini. See Chigi Saracini.
Sárai, Tibor, 54
Sartori, Claudio, 54, 150, 162
Sass, Herbert, 119
Sauer, Wilhelm, 83
Saunders, Percy, 149
Saunders, Rosamond, 131
Scanzoni, Signe von, 74
Scarlatti, Alessandro, 86
Scarlatti, Domenico, 51, 94
Schaal, Richard, 56, 72, 73, 108, 125
Schanppecher, Melchior (Malcior of Worms), 46